Teaching Family Child Care Record Keeping and Tax Preparation:

A Curriculum for Trainers

by Tom Copeland, JD

ISBN: 1-884834-63-9

Published by:
Redleaf Press
a division of Resources for Child Caring
450 N. Syndicate, Suite 5
St. Paul, MN 55104
(651) 641-6675

Policy on duplication and distribution of handouts in this curriculum:
Handouts in this curriculum may be distributed in training workshops provided that no fee is charged for any handouts, including any costs to reproduce them.

Disclaimer:
This publication is being sold with the understanding that Redleaf Press and the author are not engaged in rendering legal, accounting, or other professional services. If you require legal or tax assistance, obtain the services of a qualified professional.

Acknowledgments

MW00806084

Thanks to Thomas Lukaszewski (CPA), Sandy Schroeder (EA), and Connie Bettis (Cooperative Extension Specialist) for reviewing the earlier edition of this curriculum and providing helpful feedback. Thanks also to American Express for funding the earlier edition of this curriculum.

Redleaf National Institute

Redleaf National Institute is the national center for the business of family child care. The Institute is directed by Tom Copeland, a licensed attorney and the author of *The Basic Guide to Family Child Care Record Keeping,* the annual *Family Child Care Tax Workbook,* and *Family Child Care Contracts and Policies: How to Be Businesslike in a Caring Profession.* Our mission is to improve the quality of family child care by delivering high-quality products and services that strengthen the ability of providers to successfully manage their business. Redleaf National Institute offers the following services:

- Training workshops for family child care providers on record keeping, taxes, marketing, legal issues, contracts and policies, and money management and retirement.

- Training workshops for trainers on how to teach family child care record keeping and taxes.

- Training workshops for tax preparers on the unique tax rules affecting family child care clients.

- Technical assistance provided by telephone, fax, or E-mail on all business-related issues for family child care providers, tax preparers, and organizations that support family child care providers.

- Help for providers who are audited by the Internal Revenue Service.

- Telephone consulting on how to defend against an audit, how to best support your case, and how to appeal the decision. We can also send relevant IRS court decisions and rulings that may help a provider. We have successfully represented numerous providers in audits, on appeal, and in Tax Court.

- Advocacy on behalf of family child care. We have successfully lobbied the IRS to clarify several tax issues dealing with the Time-Space percentage and food deductions.

For further information about these services, contact Redleaf National Institute, 450 North Syndicate, Suite 5, St. Paul, MN 55104, phone: 651-641-6675, fax: 651-645-0990, e-mail: fzpg63a@prodigy.com.

Contents

Introduction to the Curriculum

Teaching Family Child Care Record Keeping and Tax Preparation is written for three groups of people—those who are training or want to start training family child care providers on the subject of record keeping and tax preparation, tax preparers who serve family child care clients and conduct training sessions either as a service to their community or as a way to attract more clients, and those who want to know more about record keeping and taxes so they can better answer the questions of family child care providers.

This curriculum will help make you a better trainer of family child care providers, whether you are a private consultant, a teacher, an active or former child care provider, a new or experienced instructor, or a trainer who works for child care resource and referral agencies, Child and Adult Care Food Program sponsors, educational institutions (technical colleges, universities, private colleges), or various support organizations for small businesses. *Teaching Family Child Care Record Keeping and Tax Preparation* tells you how to teach and what subjects should be emphasized. No previous experience or special training is necessary to use this curriculum. However, readers must have copies of two other books, both published by Redleaf Press, that are referenced in this curriculum. They are *The Basic Guide to Family Child Care Record Keeping* (5th edition) and the *Family Child Care Tax Workbook* (latest annual edition). These two books contain all of the content you will need to teach record keeping and tax preparation.

This curriculum is divided into three chapters. Chapter 1 contains a series of general teaching tips and strategies to help you become a more effective teacher and to handle problems that arise in family child care workshops. Chapter 2 divides the subject of record keeping and tax preparation into six major training units—The Basics of Record Keeping, The Time-Space Percentage, Business Expenses, Hiring Helpers, Depreciation, and Miscellaneous Topics. The training units are designed so they can be taught separately or all together. They can be taught in any order, although they are presented in a suggested order. The six training units are then further divided into four sections:

"**Key Points to Cover**" summarizes the essential points that you should cover when teaching this unit. Each of these key points is highlighted on the accompanying handouts. You may want to review this section just before your workshop or use it as the outline for your presentation.

"**Teaching Techniques**" offers a number of suggestions for how you can most effectively present the subject matter in a workshop. It includes practical advice about how you can make the topic understandable and examples of how to illustrate a point by writing on a blackboard or flip chart.

"**Commonly Asked Questions**" identifies some typical questions that workshop participants may ask. Use this section to better prepare yourself and to better understand the audience.

"**Background Notes for the Trainer**" provides a broader understanding of the subject area by describing IRS policies and the practical experience of tax preparers and audits.

Each training unit contains a series of handouts that are designed for a variety of uses. You may reproduce some or all of them and distribute them to workshop participants. You might also want to copy them onto a blackboard or use them on an overhead projector as a teaching aid. You can also use the handouts as your own outline for teaching. Chapter 3 offers suggestions as to what might be reasonably covered in workshops of one, two, and three hours in length. To some extent, the style of each trainer, the size of the audience, and the number of questions asked dictate how long it will take to teach each unit. This chapter also describes how to promote and evaluate your training workshops. The appendix contains lists of IRS forms and publications that family child care providers often use, as well as selected articles and rulings pertinent to the family child care business.

Chapter 1

General Teaching Techniques

Introduction

Understanding family child care record keeping and tax preparation and teaching this subject to others are not necessarily the same thing. This chapter covers a number of techniques to help you improve your ability to teach and communicate with family child care providers. Most of these techniques can be used effectively in teaching a variety of topics to providers. These techniques are offered as suggestions; trainers may need to adapt them to a specific situation.

The most important principle in effective teaching of record keeping and tax preparation to family child care providers is to talk to the audience in a language they can understand. Many trainers make the mistake of using technical IRS language (*business basis, allocation, net profit, accelerated depreciation,* for example) without explaining the meanings of these words. Some trainers talk on and on without taking the time to field questions and gauge the audience's comprehension of what they are saying. Be sure to listen to your audience. The teaching techniques in this chapter should help in this regard. Make an effort to learn as much as you can about family child care providers, including spending time in providers' homes to see what goes on.

No matter how experienced, every trainer should start the workshop by stating to the audience that, as a trainer, you are not giving out professional advice. You are sharing general tax knowledge and are not advising particular individuals about how to fill out their tax returns. Providers should always be advised to consult with a professional advisor (such as a tax preparer, Certified Public Accountant, Enrolled Agent, or attorney) for help in applying general tax principles to their specific situation. Here is an example of a disclaimer you may want to use:

"Before I begin this workshop I'd like to issue this disclaimer. I am not providing legal, accounting, or other professional services. I am teaching general tax and record-keeping principles. I am not providing professional advice for your particular tax circumstances. If you want professional assistance, consult a tax professional."

The Physical Setup of the Room

Participants at workshops on record keeping and tax preparation need to take written notes to remember the information. When possible, it is best for the audience to sit at tables so they can take notes easily. There is no perfect setup for the placement of chairs and tables. Some sample setups are shown below.

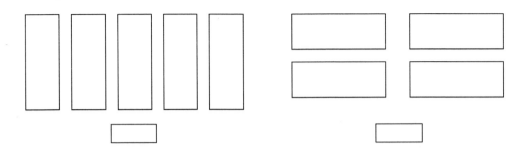

Set up a small table in the front for your notes and copies of any handouts, books, or other materials. Invite the audience to come up during breaks or at the end to look at what you have brought. This encourages participants to ask you additional questions. Be careful to distinguish between materials that participants can take for free and those which must be paid for or are only for reference.

Before you begin, ask if everyone can hear you clearly. You may have to use a microphone or encourage those in the back to move closer. If the room conditions make it hard for everyone to hear someone asking you a question, repeat the question before answering it.

Many trainers find that it is an absolute necessity to have something to write on that the class participants can see (for example, a blackboard, white board, flip chart, overhead projector). Use the visual aid to illustrate examples in your presentation and to show calculations. You can have transparencies made of the handouts at the end of each unit and display them on an overhead projector or write out parts of them on a blackboard.

Try to stand as close to the audience as possible. Do not stand on a raised platform unless the audience is so large that you can't be seen otherwise. The less distance you put between yourself and your audience, the less intimidating you will be. This is important because the topic of record keeping and taxes can be threatening to many. Being physically accessible will help reduce the tension in the room and make it easier for participants to ask questions.

For classes one to two-and-a-half hours long, breaks may or may not be necessary. Ask the sponsor or the class participants if they want a break. If the audience has some control over breaks, they will generally be more attentive. If the class is three hours or longer, plan at least a fifteen minute break in the middle. Any longer than fifteen minutes tends to make it harder for the audience to come back with their full attention. If your audience seems tired or restless, take a short break, even if you hadn't planned one.

Teaching Family Child Care Record Keeping and Tax Preparation

Preliminary Matters—Breaking the Ice

Try to begin on time, even if this means a few people will miss part of the workshop. Show respect for those who are on time rather than rewarding those who are late. Because of the serious nature of the topic, providers who come to workshops on record keeping and taxes are usually nervous at first. They will also tend to view any presenter with some suspicion and fear, especially if the presenter is male. To help reduce this initial anxiety, consider taking the following steps at the start of your workshop:

1) Briefly introduce yourself. Where you can, point out what you have in common with the audience or what your experience is with providers (for example, you are a provider, a former provider, have used a provider, visited a family child care home, trained many providers, appreciate the work of providers, and so on).

2) Find out a little about the audience. Ask the audience some questions to learn more about them and why they are attending. These questions can also be used to help you evaluate the audience's level of expertise. Ask for a show of hands: How many have been in business for one year? five years? ten years? more than ten years? How many use tax preparers? How many are group home providers? How many hire helpers? How many are tax preparers?

3) Write on the board a short list of the four to six areas you will cover in your presentation. Review this agenda with the audience. Ask, "Are there other issues you want covered?" or "Does anyone have a question now that they don't think will be covered by this agenda?" If anyone does have a question that will be covered later, reassure that person that the question will be answered. Sometimes a person has a burning question and won't be able to listen closely to you until they know that their question will be answered. If a question is asked in an area that you hadn't planned to cover, you can choose to add it to the agenda, or tell the person you will answer it at the break or after the class.

4) If the audience can't think of any questions at the start, tell them that they can raise a new topic at any time during your presentation. When such questions come up later, you can decide whether or not to handle them at that point.

5) Don't hold questions until you are finished with a topic. Invite the audience to ask questions throughout your talk. This requires you to think more quickly and to remember where you stopped in your presentation. As a general rule, the more you encourage questions, the more comfortable the audience will feel.

6) Some trainers like to start their presentation by telling a joke. Humor can build an emotional link with the audience, but be careful not to offend anyone. Making a joke at the expense of the IRS or a tax preparer may help the audience relax. Closely observe the audience's reaction to your joke. If it makes the audience more tense, don't repeat the joke at your next presentation.

How to Deal with Too Few Questions

Workshop participants learn the most when they can ask questions freely. A general rule of thumb is that you should not speak longer than ten minutes without fielding a question. If your audience isn't asking questions it may mean that they are confused by what you are saying, intimidated about asking questions, or perhaps they just aren't listening.

If you aren't interrupted by questions, you must do more to let the audience know you want them to ask questions. Before moving on to a new topic, ask, "Are there any questions?" Count silently to ten before proceeding. To help the audience relax during this pause, you must be relaxed yourself. To do so, take a drink of water, erase something from the board, sit down, or smile at the audience. It is important to wait a few moments in silence because this will encourage questions. Other things to say to encourage questions:

"I can't believe that everything I have said so far is perfectly clear. If you don't understand something, please ask me about it now. Some of the material we will cover later is more complicated, so speak up now."

"It's okay to ask questions. I'll be happy to answer any question, no matter how simple you may believe it is."

"Is there a question from the left (right) side of the room? I haven't heard many questions from this area so far."

If the audience is generally silent and unresponsive, you may want to ask, "What are people thinking about?" This may uncover some hidden question or agenda that someone in the audience may have, even if it is totally unrelated to what you are covering at the moment.

The audience will be more relaxed and ready to ask questions if they have an opportunity to share their experiences. To encourage this, pose questions such as, "How many people have ever claimed more in food expenses than they received from the Food Program?" or "How many people have been told not to depreciate your home?" or "How many people file quarterly estimated tax forms?" Then ask someone who raises their hand to explain their situation. Once a few people begin sharing, others will usually follow.

How to Deal with Questions You Can't Answer

No trainer has an answer for every question. Here are some strategies to address this problem:

Admit that you don't know the answer. Don't pretend to know something you don't. Your audience will only be upset if you mislead them, rather than if you admit you don't know. It is okay not to know everything.

If you can't remember the answer right away or if you think you can quickly find the answer by looking it up, tell the person you will try to answer it after the break or at the end of the class.

Tell the person they need to ask their tax preparer or call the local IRS office.

Tell the person you will get back to them in a few days if they will give you their phone number.

Ask if someone else in the audience knows the answer. If someone does give an answer and you suspect it may be wrong, tell the audience that you can't confirm the answer given.

How to Deal with Someone Asking Too Many Questions

It is usually a very positive sign when an audience is asking a lot of questions. If you get many questions on a particular subject, it may mean that you need to take more time to explain things carefully. If someone came in late or wasn't listening carefully and asks a question that was answered earlier, you may either give the answer again (if it can be done in a few words) or say, "I covered that question earlier, but I'd be happy to stay afterward and answer it then."

If one person is asking many questions and monopolizing the discussion, others in the audience may grow restless or not pay as close attention. If this starts to happen, you may want to say:

"I'd like to answer a question from someone who hasn't spoken up yet. Who has a question?"

"Who has a question from the other side of the room?"

"I'd love to answer your questions, but I'd like to give other people an opportunity to ask a question." (Spoken to the person who is asking many questions.)

"I can't take the time right now to answer all your questions because we have to move on to another subject, but if you'd like to stay after, I would be happy to talk to you then." (Again, spoken to the person who is asking many questions.)

In addition, you could move your body slightly so the person asking the questions is outside of your direct line of sight. This makes it easier for you to see others who may wish to ask questions and to move away from the person who is monopolizing the discussion.

How to Make Sure Your Audience Understands You

Telling is not the same thing as teaching, and listening is not the same thing as learning. Record keeping and tax preparation are not inherently exciting or popular topics to teach. Audiences can get confused, bored, or exhausted listening to all the complex IRS rules. Here are some tips to help your audience comprehend what you are saying.

Whenever possible, give examples. Use the blackboard, overhead projector, or handouts to illustrate your point. Ask the audience to supply the facts for your example. For instance, if you are discussing house repairs, ask for examples of real house repairs from the audience. Before moving on to a new topic, stop and ask if there are any more questions about what you've just covered.

Periodically, you may want to ask short questions to test if your audience is understanding you. For example: "What's the most important thing to remember about claiming food expenses?" (Save all the receipts) or "Should you report Food Program reimbursements as income?" (Yes) or "Should you use your Time-Space percentage in depreciating your TV?" (No).

After responding to a complex question, it is useful to ask the question, "Did you understand my answer?" Give the person who asked the question an opportunity to follow up with another question. Also, when explaining a difficult subject such as depreciation, ask the question, "Does this make sense?" Watch for audience reactions. If they are nodding their heads or looking directly at you, this usually means the audience understands what you are saying.

Make sure you are making the audience comfortable enough to ask questions. If people in the audience are talking among themselves a lot, it may be a sign that they are confused. If so, go back and give a more simple explanation than you first offered. Ask, "What don't you understand?" Try not to leave a topic when many in the audience are still confused. If only a few don't seem to be following you, offer to stay after the workshop to explain the topic in more detail.

If your audience is becoming overwhelmed by all the complex IRS rules, try not to go into too much detail on particular topics. Stick to the highlights and use the "Key Points to Cover" for each unit in chapter 2. Reassure the audience that no one expects them to remember every rule and that they can consult the handouts, Redleaf Press books, IRS publications, or their tax preparer for further information.

How to Explain the Uncertainties of Tax Laws

Not all IRS rules and regulations can be easily explained with concrete statements. Sometimes it may be difficult to logically explain a tax rule that seems unfair or just plain stupid. But remember, your role as a trainer is not to justify IRS rules, it is to explain them. Instead of defending the validity of IRS rules, you can say, "We may not like this rule, but it is the law" or "This rule may seem unfair or overly complicated, but I want everyone to understand what the IRS will do in this situation if you are audited."

There are many situations that cannot be explained with a simple yes or no answer. For example: "May I deduct the mileage to the grocery store when I buy business and personal food?" or "May I deduct the cost of my garden supplies?" In these situations, try to explain how the answer can depend on the particular facts and circumstances of each case. Give specific facts that will cause your answer to be yes and then change the facts so the answer will be no. For example, here is an answer to the question "May I deduct my sewing machine?": If you used your sewing machine on a regular basis to make clothes for the children in your care (or to make other items for the business), then you could claim part of the cost of the sewing machine as a business expense. Use your Time-Space percentage (or an actual business-use percent) and depreciate the cost. If you only use your sewing machine for personal purposes, don't claim any expense for your business.

Sometimes IRS rules are interpreted differently by IRS agents and tax preparers. Explain that providers may have some room to argue their position to the IRS. The more records and evidence a provider can bring forth, the more convincing the argument will be. In areas of tax law that are uncertain, providers should be encouraged to take a reasonable position about claiming deductions and not worry about being second guessed.

Teaching Family Child Care Record Keeping and Tax Preparation

## Chapter 2

Curriculum Training Units

Unit A: The Basics of Record Keeping

Introduction

This unit covers how to explain the key principles of good record keeping for the family child care business. The contents of this unit are the foundation on which all tax training should be built. Every workshop you teach should include something from this unit. Saving proper records is the single most important message to communicate to providers. A comprehensive explanation of the basic rules of record keeping can be found in *The Basic Guide to Family Child Care Record Keeping*. The *Calendar-Keeper* is a record-keeping system that tracks income and expenses for providers. It is published by Redleaf Press and updated annually. In addition, IRS **Publication 587 Business Use of Your Home** contains additional information about record keeping.

Key Points to Cover

Providers need to keep accurate records for all income received and receipts for all business expenses (see Handout 1). This is the most important point to stress when teaching record keeping. Providers should understand that as self-employed business owners, they must file tax forms each year. The more complete and accurate their record keeping, the better providers will be able to reduce their taxes and increase their profits.

Handout 2 lists the seven most important record-keeping rules. Emphasize that these rules are absolutely critical in order to meet IRS expectations. Providers who obey these major rules will be in a position to maximize their profits.

One of the purposes of record keeping is to keep business records separate from personal records (see Handout 3). Having a separate checkbook for the business is a useful idea, but it is not required. Business records should be organized by expense category (rather than by month), since that is the way expenses will be totaled at the end of the year. Record keeping is a year-round job. Records must be saved for three years after the tax return is filed. Records for items that are being depreciated (for example, house, home improvements, play equipment, vehicle, appliances, and furniture) must be kept for their depreciation life plus three years. For example, if a stove purchased in 1998 is depreciated over eight years, records on the purchase of the stove must be saved until 2009.

Providers must keep track of all sources of income during the year (see Handout 4) and be able to know how much was received from each parent (see Handout 5). Many professional providers give parents a payment receipt to establish an accurate income record (see Handout 6). Such a receipt can be given each time a parent pays, or one receipt can be given at the end of the year.

Parents who wish to claim the federal child care tax credit (using **Form 2441 Child and Dependent Care Expenses**) must obtain their provider's name, address, and Social Security number (or taxpayer identification number) from **Form W-10 Dependent Care Provider's Identification and Certification**. It is the parent's responsibility—not the provider's—to get this form. If the provider refuses to fill it out, the provider is subject to a $50 penalty. Many providers, as a courtesy, fill out **Form W-10** and give it to parents before being asked to do so (see Handout 7).

Providers will not know what parents are recording on **Form 2441**. They may inflate the amount of money that they claim to have paid you for child care. To protect themselves from an audit, providers should keep their own accurate records of how much each parent paid.

Providers should save receipts for all business expenses, including all expenses associated with cleaning, repairing, and improving the house. If the receipt doesn't say clearly what the expense is for, providers should mark what it is on the receipt. If a receipt is lost or was never received, re-create the receipt as soon as possible after the purchase. Document items purchased before going into business by photographing or videotaping them (see Handout 8).

Keeping track of business food expenses is probably the most difficult record-keeping task (see guidelines in Handout 9). To estimate food expenses, follow this three-step process: 1) Save all food receipts (business and personal); 2) calculate an average cost per serving using several meals as example; and 3) multiply by the number of meals served. There are many ways providers can calculate business food expenses (see Handouts 10, 11, and 12).

Providers are always better off financially by joining the Child and Adult Care Food Program. Trainers and tax preparers should encourage every provider to join. (See Handouts 13 and 14).

Food Program reimbursements for a provider's own children are not taxable income. Handout 15 shows how to calculate how much a provider received for her own children. Adjust the reimbursement rates after July 1 of each year.

Teaching Techniques

Use the *Calendar-Keeper* or similar record-keeping calendar to illustrate how providers can organize their records. Show the Attendance and Payment Log pages and the Expense pages for each month as an example of how to keep track of income and expenses. Some providers may want to use a notebook or computer software program to record income and expenses. Bring several large envelopes labeled with the various categories of business expenses (for example, "food," "utilities," "education," and "supplies") to show how records can be organized. In an audit, the IRS usually asks to see all checkbooks and savings accounts. They are looking for unreported income. Providers should be strongly encouraged to identify the source of each deposit (for example, "child care income," "husband's paycheck," "reimbursement for mileage from husband's employer"). Unaccounted for deposits are likely to be treated as business income (which is taxed at a higher rate than personal income).

When discussing the importance of keeping all business receipts, it may be helpful to make this comparison: The worst model is a provider who has no records or receipts and is putting down wild estimates on her tax return, and the best model is a provider who has every receipt clearly marked and can back up each number on her tax return. Most providers are probably somewhere between these two extremes. The message to communicate is that providers should try to move closer each year to the second provider's example. Each additional receipt that a provider can save is a step in the right direction.

Purchase a sales receipt book from a drug store or stationery store and bring it to your workshops. Use this sales book to show providers how it can be used to get receipts at garage sales or other places that don't issue receipts. The provider should make sure the receipt contains the following information: date of sale, address, description of item, cost, payment method, and signature of seller (if possible).

Many providers are not aware of all the house-related expenses that are deductible. Give some examples of such expenses, including lightbulbs, toilet paper, paper towels, window cleaner, laundry soap, broom, hammer, and nails. Encourage providers to save all receipts when shopping at a hardware store or drug store because many of these expenses will be at least partially deductible.

Sometimes providers are surprised to learn about their responsibility to keep accurate records. Encourage them by saying that it's never too late to begin keeping records. If a provider has not kept records for several months, tell her she can reconstruct records for those months and that she should start now to develop the good habits of record keeping.

If your audience is feeling discouraged about the difficulty and complexity of record keeping, ask for a participant to volunteer how she keeps track of food receipts or other expenses. Many providers have developed their own methods that work. Use the answers given by these providers as an illustration that accurate record keeping can be done and that there is more than one way to accomplish this. Using successful examples from the audience creates a positive atmosphere and is an effective way to communicate this subject.

Many providers do not keep accurate records of their business food expenses. To illustrate the benefits of keeping accurate records of these expenses, ask those in the audience to share how they calculate their business food expenses. Comment on these examples as to whether the providers are doing enough to support their claims (for example, one provider doesn't save her attendance records). To encourage providers to claim more than just the amount of their reimbursement from the CACFP, ask these questions: "How many of you claim more in food expenses than you received from the Food Program?" "How many of you claim less?" In most cases, the majority will say they claim more. Use this fact to point out that this is common and that many who don't claim more in food expenses than they received from the Food Program are probably cheating themselves—they are claiming too little. Those providers who pay closer attention to tracking their food expenses are likely to be claiming higher expenses and paying less taxes.

To reinforce the rule that providers should be saving personal as well as business food receipts, read the following sentence from **Publication 587 Business Use of Your Home:** "If you deduct the cost of food for your day-care business, keep a separate record (with receipts) of your family's food costs." Many providers are surprised to learn this.

Commonly Asked Questions

Is it my responsibility to track down parents who left earlier in the year and give them Form W-10?

No. If a parent doesn't present **Form W-10** to you, you have no responsibility to track down the parent. It is a good idea to have parents sign a receipt when they leave, indicating how much they paid for the year. Keep a copy of this receipt for your records.

With each parent, I write on Form W-10 how much they paid me for the year. Doesn't this protect me from a parent who is thinking about claiming more on their Form 2441?

Not always. It is best to have the parent sign your **Form W-10** and keep a copy for your own records.

A parent left earlier in the year owing me $200. Now the parent has called and asked me to fill out Form W-10. Is there anything I can do?

You could tell the parent that you won't fill out the form until you receive the $200. You might want to delay filling out the form until April to put pressure on the parent. In the end, your liability for refusing to fill out the **Form W-10** is only $50.

I have heard about some providers who charge parents a lower rate if the parents agree not to claim their child care tax credit. Should I consider doing this?

Providers who make this kind of agreement with parents are not reporting their income to the IRS and are taking a chance. If the IRS audits them, they will owe back taxes, interest, and possibly penalties. Providers are responsible for reporting all their income to the IRS. You can charge parents whatever you want. Providers will be better off in the long run if they report their income and claim all the deductions that the law allows.

What should I do if I lose a receipt or forget to get one when I purchase something?

As soon as you realize you don't have a receipt, take these steps to reconstruct your records: Save any check stubs or credit card bills, take a picture of the item, and create a receipt with all the relevant information. It is not acceptable to write out 150 "new" receipts on December 31.

Must I report reimbursements from the Food Program as income?

Although the IRS has issued some confusing advice on this question, the best advice is to report it as income and claim all business food expenses as deductions on **Schedule C Profit and Loss from Business.**

Isn't it better not to join the Food Program if the income pushes me into a higher tax bracket?

No. If this happens to you, you will only pay a higher tax on the small amount of income that is in the higher tax bracket. You will still be better off financially by joining the Food Program.

May I claim the food that I eat while caring for children?

No. **Publication 587 Business Use of Your Home** (1997 edition) says, "You can never deduct the cost of food consumed by you or your family."

May I use my Time-Space percentage to calculate my food deductions?

No. The Time-Space percentage has nothing to do with the consumption of food.

If I write a check to myself from my business checkbook, is this a business expense?

No. This is paying yourself for your work and represents the profit from your business. Do not record it as an expense.

Background Notes for the Trainer

IRS audits are usually won on the basis of how accurately and completely the provider kept records. And the appearance of accurate records is often just as important as the records themselves. While providers should be told that there aren't any shortcuts to keeping accurate records, they should also be encouraged to do the best job they can and not give up. Many providers have successfully won audits by arguing their case and using reconstructed records.

The IRS has begun to use its computers to match what providers are reporting as income on **Schedule C** with what parents are reporting as child care expenses on **Form 2441**. Providers are likely to be audited if these numbers don't match. Parents may make mistakes on their **Form 2441** by putting the child care payments for several providers in one year under the Social Security number of their latest provider. As long as providers have accurate records of parent payments (and, ideally, signed receipts), they should not worry.

The IRS is writing an audit guide on family child care. In it they point out that many providers underreport their income and do not keep careful business records. Redleaf Press will publish this guide when it becomes available.

Food program sponsors do not need to issue **Form 1099 Miscellaneous Income** to their providers.

The IRS clarified its position on reporting Food Program reimbursements and food expenses in the 1995 edition of **Publication 587 Business Use of Your Home.** This publications states:

> Reimbursements you receive from a sponsor under the Child and Adult Food Care Program of the Department of Agriculture are only taxable to the extent they exceed your expenses for food for eligible children. If your reimbursements are more than your expenses for food, show the difference as income in Part I of **Schedule C.** If your food expenses are greater than the reimbursements, show the difference as an expense in Part V of **Schedule C.** Do not include payments or expenses for your own children if they are eligible for the program. Follow this procedure even if you receive a **Form 1099** reporting a payment from the sponsor.

The biggest problem most providers face is trying to separate their business food expense from their personal food expense. A simple and accurate method to calculate business food expenses is to use the cost per meal method (see Handout 10).

Despite its recommendation that only the net income or expenses should be reported, the best advice continues to be to report both income and expenses. Note that **Publication 587** also says that reimbursements for the provider's own children are not taxable income.

Food is probably the most commonly audited expense. Some auditors allow providers to claim only what they get from the Food Program as an expense. This is not the law and providers should be encouraged to fight this position. The best way to show food income and expenses on **Schedule C** is to report Food Program income as "Other Income" (line 6) and list food expenses as "Other Expenses" (line 27).

As a last resort, providers who have not saved adequate food receipts should report expenses equal to the Food Program's per meal reimbursement rate (Tier I) multiplied by the number of meals and children they serve (including nonreimbursed meals).* Although the IRS may challenge this estimate, providers should be able to reconstruct enough records (number of meals served, attendance, menus) to support this position.

---

*As of July 1997 the Food Program has two reimbursement rates for providers. The higher Tier I rate is for low-income providers, providers who live in a low-income area, and providers who serve low-income children. Providers who don't meet one of these tests receive the lower Tier II rate. For purposes of calculating food deductions, however, providers should use the higher Tier I rate.

The Importance of Record Keeping

- Family child care providers are self-employed taxpayers who run a business out of their own home.

- The reasons for keeping complete and accurate records are

    1) to obey the law by filing your business tax forms each year,

    2 to be able to support your tax claims for business expenses,

    3) to reduce your taxes and increase your profit, and

    4) to make it easier for you to understand your business and reach your financial goals.

© Redleaf National Institute, *Teaching Family Child Care Record Keeping and Tax Preparation: A Curriculum for Trainers* (St. Paul: Redleaf Press, 1998), 1-800-423-8309.

The Seven Rules of Good Record Keeping

1) Track income from each parent and the Child and Adult Care Food Program.

2) Save the receipts for all business purchases.

3) Mark what each item is on the receipt.

4) Organize receipts by category, not month.

5) Keep track of how much time each week you use your home for your business.

6) Conduct a regular review (at least monthly) of your records.

7) After filing your tax return, keep your records in a safe place for 3 years.

© Redleaf National Institute, *Teaching Family Child Care Record Keeping and Tax Preparation: A Curriculum for Trainers* (St. Paul: Redleaf Press, 1998), 1-800-423-8309.

Checkbooks and Storing Records

- Try to keep your business records as separate as possible from your personal records.

- Establish a business account and checkbook separate from your personal account. Use the account to deposit your business income and to pay for business expenses.

- Identify the source of funds for all deposits in personal checking and savings accounts.

- Organize all receipts by expense category and keep them in a safe place.

Sources of Business Income

1) Parent fees.

2) Child and Adult Care Food Program reimbursements.

3) Government subsidies for low-income parents.

4) Grants from government or private agencies to purchase equipment or make home improvements.

Tracking Parent Fees

- Keep accurate records showing how much each parent paid you for your services and how many hours you provided care for each child.

- Here are two methods of keeping records of parent income:

JUNE ATTENDANCE AND PAYMENT LOG

CHILD'S NAME	S	M	T	W	T	F	S 1	TOTAL	S 2	M 3	T 4	W 5	T 6	F 7	S 8	TOTAL	S 9	M 1
Alisha										X	X	X	X	X		$80		
Francis										X		X		X		$50		
Albert										X	X	X	X	X		$70		
Shanna										X	X	X	X	X		$80		

WEEKLY PAYMENT TOTALS $280

Week of January 1, 1999

Mrs. Nicol   M-F   8-5 $80 pd
Mrs. Sobin   M,W,F   8-5 $50 pd
Mrs. Rogers   M-F   8-5 $70 pd
Mrs. Lombardi   M-F   8-5 $80 pd
$280

© Redleaf National Institute, *Teaching Family Child Care Record Keeping and Tax Preparation: A Curriculum for Trainers* (St. Paul: Redleaf Press, 1998), 1-800-423-8309.

Parent Receipts

- Give parents a receipt to establish an accurate income record for your business.

- Give parents a receipt each time they make a payment, or give them one receipt at the end of the year.

- Parents should sign each receipt. Both parent and provider should keep a copy.

- Receipts are especially important when parents pay cash.

Examples of receipts:

BUSINESS RECEIPT FOR CHILD CARE SERVICES   ©1990 Redleaf Press, St. Paul, MN

No. _45_   3/19 19 99

Received from _John and Madelyne Crawford_ $ 85.00
                (parent/guardian name)

Eighty-five Dollars and no/100 _____ Dollars

☐ Cash
☒ Check # _2430_   **For Child Care Services** from _3 12 99_ to _3 19 99_
                                              M D Y   M D Y

Provider's Signature _Anne Thomas_

Parent's Signature _Madelyne Crawford_

140753

Customer's Order No. _____   Date _1/9_ 19 _99_

Name _Mrs. Albertson_

Address

SOLD BY	CASH	C.O.D.	CHARGE	ON ACCT.	MDSE. RETD.	PAID OUT

QUAN.	DESCRIPTION	PRICE	AMOUNT
	For child care services for Jenny Albertson		
	1/1/99 - 1/8/99 Pd		$80 00
	Faye albertson		
	Joan Snader		

ALL claims and returned goods MUST be accompanied by this bill.

Rec'd by

Paid #3,800 for child care in 1999   Pat Battis

Form **W-10**   **Dependent Care Provider's Identification and Certification**

(Rev. August 1994)

Department of the Treasury
Internal Revenue Service   Do NOT file Form W-10 with your tax return. Instead, keep it for your records.

Part I   Dependent Care Provider's Identification (See instructions.)

Please print or type

Name of dependent care provider
Delores Carlos

Provider's taxpayer identification number
_123-45-6789_

Address (number, street, and apt. no.)
418 Ohawa Ave S

If the above number is a social security number, check here ▶ . . . . . . ☒

City, state, and ZIP code
Bisbee, Arizona 85603

Certification and Signature of Dependent Care Provider.—Under penalties of perjury, I, as the dependent care provider, certify that my name, address, and taxpayer identification number shown above are correct.

Please Sign Here

Dependent care provider's signature
Delores Carlos

Date
_1/1/2000_

Part II   Name and Address of Person Requesting Part I Information (See instructions.)

Name, street address, apt. no., city, state, and ZIP code of person requesting information
Pat Battis, Bisbee, Arizona 85603
_21 W 50th St_

© Redleaf National Institute, *Teaching Family Child Care Record Keeping and Tax Preparation: A Curriculum for Trainers* (St. Paul: Redleaf Press, 1998), 1-800-423-8309.

Form W-10 and the Child Care Tax Credit

- If parents wish to claim the child care tax credit on **Form 2441 Child and Dependent Care Expenses,** they must have the provider's name, address, and Social Security number (or taxpayer identification number).

- It is the parent's responsibility—not the provider's—to obtain **Form W-10** and ask the provider to fill it out.

- Providers are subject to a penalty of $50 for each **Form W-10** they refuse to fill out.

Paid #3,000 for child care in 1999 Polly Parent

Form W-10

(Rev. August 1994)

Department of the Treasury
Internal Revenue Service

Dependent Care Provider's Identification and Certification

Do NOT file Form W-10 with your tax return. Instead, keep it for your records.

Part I Dependent Care Provider's Identification (See instructions.)

Please print or type

Name of dependent care provider
Doreen Provider

Provider's taxpayer identification number
311-64-7891

Address (number, street, and apt. no.)
123 Baldwin Street

If the above number is a social security number, check here ▶ . . . . . . ☒

City, state, and ZIP code
St Paul, Mn 55104

Certification and Signature of Dependent Care Provider.—Under penalties of perjury, I, as the dependent care provider, certify that my name, address, and taxpayer identification number shown above are correct.

Please Sign Here

Dependent care provider's signature
Doreen Provider

Date
1-1-2000

Part II Name and Address of Person Requesting Part I Information (See instructions.)

Name, street address, apt. no., city, state, and ZIP code of person requesting information
Polly Parent 456 Target Lane St Paul, Mn 55110

Form 2441

Department of the Treasury
Internal Revenue Service (T)

Child and Dependent Care Expenses

▶ Attach to Form 1040.

▶ See separate instructions.

OMB No. 1545-0068

199

Attachment
Sequence No. **21**

Name(s) shown on Form 1040
Polly Parent

Your social security number
543 78 4620

You need to understand the following terms to complete this form: **Qualifying Person(s), Dependent Care Benefits, Qualified Expenses,** and **Earned Income.** See **Important Terms** on page 1 of the Form 2441 instructions.

Part I Persons or Organizations Who Provided the Care—You **must** complete this part.
(If you need more space, use the bottom of page 2.)

1	(a) Care provider's name	(b) Address (number, street, apt. no., city, state, and ZIP code)	(c) Identifying number (SSN or EIN)	(d) Amount paid (see instructions)
	Doreen Provider	*123 Baldwin St. St Paul, Mn 53104*	*311-64-7891*	*$3 000*

2	Add the amounts in column (d) of line 1	2	*3,000*

© Redleaf National Institute, *Teaching Family Child Care Record Keeping and Tax Preparation: A Curriculum for Trainers* (St. Paul: Redleaf Press, 1998), 1-800-423-8309.

Keeping Track of Expenses

- Save all receipts of direct expenses for your business, including receipts for food, toys, supplies, and diapers.

- Save all receipts associated with the cleaning, repair, and improvement of your house, including receipts for items such as a broom, hammer, garden hose, and lightbulbs.

- A partial record is better than no record. Recreate a receipt if you were not given one, forgot to get one, or lost it. For example, if you purchase a high chair at a garage sale, you might use the following receipt:

- If a receipt is not specific enough, make clarifications by writing explanatory notes directly on the receipt. For example, if a receipt just lists dollar amounts and doesn't indicate items, write the name of the item next to the appropriate amount. Or if you purchased some items for business purposes and some items for personal purposes, make this distinction by labeling each item as such.

Guidelines for Reporting CACFP Reimbursements and Food Deductions for Family Child Care Providers

1) Providers should keep adequate records to document CACFP reimbursements and food expenses. This includes keeping receipts of all business and personal food expenses.

2) Food eaten by a family child care provider at home is never deductible as a business expense.

3) All the food eaten by a helper of a family child care provider while caring for child care children is deductible as a business expense, provided that helper is not a family member.

4) Food eaten by a family child care provider's own children is not deductible as a business expense (however, note the following point).

5) CACFP reimbursements for a family child care provider's own children *are not* taxable income.

6) CACFP reimbursements for child care children *are* taxable income to the family child care provider.

7) The amount of money received as reimbursement from the CACFP does not represent the maximum amount that may be claimed as business food deductions by a provider. Providers who are on the CACFP are entitled to deduct as business expenses the cost of all food served in their business, even if this amount exceeds the CACFP reimbursement.

8) Providers who are not on the CACFP may claim as business expenses the cost of all the food served to child care children.

9) Recommended method of reporting on **Schedule C.**

Income	Expenses
"Other Income," Line 6 CACFP $2,500	"Other Expenses," Line 27 Food $2,800

10) Recommended method of reporting on **Schedule C** if provider's own child is on the CACFP.

Income
"Other Income," Line 6   CACFP $2,900 - $400 (own child) = $2,500

Expenses
"Other Expenses," Line 27   Food $2,800*

* Does not include food eaten by provider's own children on CACFP.

© Redleaf National Institute, *Teaching Family Child Care Record Keeping and Tax Preparation: A Curriculum for Trainers* (St. Paul: Redleaf Press, 1998), 1-800-423-8309.

Estimating Food Expenses:
Provider Cost Per Meal Method

STEP 1.
Calculate average provider meal cost using several meals served throughout the year.

	Breakfast	Lunch	Snack	Dinner
Meal #1	$0.85	$2.03	$0.55	$1.75
Meal #2	0.68	1.42	0.40	1.62
Meal #3	1.02	1.48	0.44	1.58
Meal #4	0.81	1.91	0.61	1.80
Total	$3.36	$6.84	$2.00	$6.75
	4 meals =	4 meals =	4 meals =	4 meals =
Average cost per meal	$0.84	$1.71	$0.50	$1.69

STEP 2.
Calculate number of meals served per year. Be sure to include all nonreimbursed meals.

Breakfast	Lunch	Snack	Dinner
3 children x	5 children x	5 children x	4 children x
5 breakfasts/week	5 lunches/week	10 snacks/week	1 dinner/month
x 50 weeks =	x 50 weeks =	x 50 weeks =	=
750 breakfasts	1,250 lunches	2,500 snacks	48 dinners

STEP 3.
Multiply average per meal cost by number of meals served.

Breakfast	750 x $0.84 =	$630.00
Lunch	1,250 x $1.71 =	$2,137.50
Snack	2,500 x $.50 =	$1,250.00
Dinner	48 x $1.69 =	$81.12
Total		$4,098.62

Total estimated food expense: $4,098.62

For further information see *The Basic Guide to Family Child Care Record Keeping and the Family Child Care Tax Workbook* (updated annually), both by Tom Copeland and published by Redleaf Press.

Estimating Food Expenses: Provider Cost Per Week Method

STEP 1.
Calculate cost of food for several weeks throughout the year.

	Week 1	Week 2	Week 3	Week 4
100% business food	$26.75	$31.64	$21.65	$28.46
100% personal food	61.83	72.85	58.44	71.58
Shared business and personal food	125.38	141.88	118.43	130.76
Business portion	75.21	82.43	65.29	72.19
Personal portion	50.17	59.45	53.14	58.57
Total of 100% business and business portion	$101.96	$114.07	$86.94	$100.65

STEP 2.
Calculate average cost per week.

Week 1	$101.96
Week 2	114.07
Week 3	86.94
Week 4	100.65

$403.62 ÷ 4 weeks = $100.91 average cost per week

STEP 3.
Multiply average cost per week by number of weeks in business.

$100.91 average cost per week x 50 weeks = $5,045.50

Total estimated food expense: $5,045.50

Estimating Food Expenses: Food Program Cost Per Meal Method

STEP 1.
Determine amount of reimbursement from the Food Program (but do not include any reimbursement for provider's own child).

> Food Program reimbursement: $3,000

STEP 2.
Calculate the number of extra meals served, but not reimbursed by the Food Program.

> An average of one extra snack that is not reimbursed by the Food Program is served each day to three children.
> 1 nonreimbursed snack x 3 children per day = 3 snacks per day
> 3 snacks per day x 5 days per week = 15 snacks per week
> 15 snacks per week x 50 weeks = 750 snacks per year

STEP 3.
Multiply the number of extra meals served by the Food Program reimbursement rate. Remember to take into account the changing reimbursement rates as of July 1 of each year. Most providers should use the Tier I rate because it more accurately reflects their actual food expense than the Tier II rate.

> January–June 1998
> Snack reimbursement rate: $0.48 (Tier I rate) x 375 snacks = $180.00
> July–December 1998
> Snack reimbursement rate $0.49 (Tier I rate) x 375 snacks = $183.75
> Total estimated cost of nonreimbursed snacks: $363.75

STEP 4.
Add amounts from Step 1 and Step 3.

> $3,000 + 363.75 = $3,363.75

Total estimated food expense: $3,363.75

Tax Consequences of Cutbacks in the Child and Adult Care Food Program Reimbursement

Some family child care providers who are not low income, who do not live in a low-income area, or do not serve low-income children will receive lower Food Program checks as of July 1997. Here are the tax consequences of such cutbacks:

	Tier I After July 1997 Food Program Payment	Tier II After July1997 Food Program Payment	Not on Food Program
Parent Fees (4 children)	$22,000	$22,000	$22,000
Food Program Reimbursements	+ 3,100[1]	+ 1,500[2]	+ 0
Total Income	25,100	23,500	22,000
Business Expenses	10,000	- 10,000	- 10,000
Food Expenses	- 3,000	- 3,000	- 3,000
Profit	12,100	10,500	9,000
Federal Taxes (40%[3])	- 4,840	- 4,200	-3,600
Cash on Hand at End of Year	**$7,260**	**$6,300**	**$5,400**

Note:
As the example shows, providers who receive lower reimbursements from the Food Program are still better off than if they receive no reimbursements. The provider in this example who remains on the Food Program will have $960 ($7,260 - $6,300) less cash on hand at the end of the year. This is still better, however, than leaving the Food Program, which would mean losing an additional $900 ($6,300 - 5,400). If you have further questions, see the *Family Child Care Tax Workbook* by Tom Copeland, published by Redleaf Press.

[1] Based on a reimbursement of $3.04 per day, for four children (1998/1999 reimbursement rate).
[2] Based on a reimbursement of $1.47 per day, for four children ($1.00 lunch and dinner, $0.34 breakfast, $0.13 snack) (1998/1999 reimbursement rate).
[3] Based on 28% federal income tax, plus 12% net Social Security tax.

Food Program Myths

Myth: I am going to be losing money because the Tier II reimbursement rate is not going to cover the cost of my food.

You are never losing money when you are on the Food Program. It's true that your reimbursement check may not pay for the food you buy for your business. But it's always better to get some money for the food you are buying than to receive nothing at all. Think of being on the Food Program like having a job. The Food Program is paying you to do some paperwork. If you were not on the Food Program you would still have to prepare a menu, buy the food, cook it, and serve it. How much are you being paid an hour for doing the paperwork required by the Food Program? If you spend three hours a week on paperwork, that is 156 hours a year. If you care for four children and receive the lower Tier II rate, you earn $1,528 a year ($382 per child x 4). Your hourly rate is $9.79 an hour ($1,528 ÷ 156 hours). If you spent less time on paperwork, your hourly earnings would go up. It is certainly worthwhile to stay on the Food Program and earn more than $9 an hour.

Myth: It's not worth it to claim a snack for only 13 cents.

Wrong. A typical provider would earn $6 an hour by claiming this snack. For example, if you claim a 13 cent snack for the entire year, the total reimbursement for one child is $33.80 ($0.13/day x 5 days/week x 52 weeks). If you care for four children and it takes five minutes a day to record these snacks, you will earn $6.24 an hour. If you spent less than five minutes to record these snacks, you will earn even more. Don't throw away this opportunity to earn more for your time than you earn caring for children.

Myth: I'll be better off if I leave the Food Program and then charge parents for food.

In order to replace money you would lose from the food program at the Tier II rate, you would have to charge parents an extra $7.35 a child each week ($382 ÷ 52 weeks). You'd have to report this income and pay taxes on it, just the same as if you received this money as a reimbursement. If you don't raise your rates by at least this much, you will be financially worse off than you were on the Food Program. If you raise your rates by $8.35 per week, you will be better off by only $1 per week. If you stay on the Food Program and raise your rates, you will keep every dollar of the increase for yourself.

Myth: I'll be better off if I leave the Food Program and then have the parents bring all the food.

While it's true that having parents bring all the food will make you better off financially, most providers cannot rely on parents to regularly bring all the food. If they don't and you spend as little as $7.85 a week per child for food (or $408 per year), then you are in the same condition as if you stayed on the Food Program at the Tier II rate. If you spend more than $408 a year for food, you will be worse off than if you stayed on the Food Program. How is this so? By having parents bring food, you are saving $790 a year in food cost per child. This assumes that you spend the same amount on food as you received from the Food Program at the Tier I $3.04 a day rate ($3.04 x 5 days x 52 weeks = $790). But you are also giving up $382 a year in food reimbursement at the Tier II level. (The Tier II rate for one child for one year is $382.) The difference is $408 a year per child ($790 [Tier I] - $382 [Tier II]). This represents your actual savings. But if you have to spend more than $408 a year on food that the parents don't bring, then you are worse off. Some parents may think it is cheaper for them to pay you $7.85 a week in higher fees so that you can remain on the Food Program and they don't have to bring all the food themselves. Also, many parents may be concerned about the nutritional quality of the food you serve their children. You could lose some parents who prefer to enroll their child with a provider who can guarantee that their child will receive nutritious meals.

Myth: Reimbursements from the Food Program are offset by my food expenses, so I'm not losing anything by leaving the program.

Wrong. You spend money on food regardless of whether or not you are on the Food Program. Most providers spend more on food than the reimbursements they receive. All food served to child care children is deductible whether or not you are on the Food Program. Any reimbursements you receive are like getting a raise or like parents paying you an extra $7.85 a week per child (Tier II rate). So leaving the Food Program is like turning down a raise or refusing to accept extra money from parents. Reimbursement from the Food Program always increases your bottom-line profit. Taking this money means the children in your care will get food that is more nutritious.

Reprinted from *Family Child Caring*, Spring 1997, © Redleaf Press.

© Redleaf National Institute, *Teaching Family Child Care Record Keeping and Tax Preparation: A Curriculum for Trainers* (St. Paul: Redleaf Press, 1998), 1-800-423-8309.

Number of Meals Served to Provider's Own Children: January 1, 1998 to June 30, 1998

	January	February	March	April	May	June	Total # of Meals	X Food Program reimbursement Rate	TOTAL
# of Breakfasts								X .88 =	$
# of Lunches								X 1.62 =	$
# of Dinners								X 1.62 =	$
# of Snacks								X .48 =	$
								A = Total	$

Number of Meals Served to Provider's Own Children: July 1, 1998 to December 31, 1998

	July	August	Sept.	Oct.	Nov.	Dec.	Total # of Meals	X Food Program reimbursement Rate*	TOTAL
# of Breakfasts								X .90 =	$
# of Lunches								X 1.65 =	$
# of Dinners								X 1.65 =	$
# of Snacks								X .49 =	$
								B = Total	$

*Tier I Rate

Unit B: The Time-Space Percentage

Introduction

This unit explains the formula providers should use to calculate the allocated house-related expenses. This formula is better known as the Time-Space percentage. Because of its importance, you may want to spend a lot of time going over the details of how to calculate the Time-Space percentage. For a comprehensive explanation of this subject, see *The Basic Guide to Family Child Care Record Keeping*. For a somewhat shorter explanation, see the *Family Child Care Tax Workbook*. You should also be familiar with IRS Revenue Ruling 92-3 (see appendix).

Key Points to Cover

The Time-Space percentage has the single greatest impact on reducing providers' taxes of any factor. Present this topic as the most important part of any record-keeping class. Because of the substantial expenses that the Time-Space percentage is applied against, stress how important it is to calculate the Time-Space percentage correctly (see Handout 1).

Focus attention on how providers can identify the maximum allowable hours they are using their home for business purposes. This is the area providers usually underestimate. Many providers, tax preparers, and auditors are not aware that providers can claim hours spent in cleaning and preparation (see Handout 2). The point to stress is the importance of keeping accurate records of hours worked (see Handout 3).

The test for whether or not the square footage of a room may be counted as business use is "if it is available for day care use for the entire day and is regularly used for day care" (IRS Revenue Ruling 92-3; see appendix). Regular use can be several hours a day (for example, a child napping in the master bedroom for two hours) or all day long (such as a playroom). A room doesn't have to be used every day (see Handout 4).

Providers who use rooms exclusively for their business can claim a higher Time-Space percentage by following the instructions found on **Form 8829 Expenses for Business Use of Your Home** (see Handout 5). Providers must enter their Time-Space percentage calculation on Part I of **Form 8829**. It must be recalculated each year.

Only after thoroughly explaining the Time-Space percentage should you introduce the concept of "actual business-use percent." Most providers use their Time-Space percentage for all shared expenses and some may be confused by this second concept. Illustrate this concept by using the example of paper towels: If a provider uses 75 percent of her paper towels for her business, she may claim 75 percent of their cost. Tell providers to save the receipts for all paper towel purchases.

Teaching Techniques

Introduce the topic of Time-Space percentage early in your workshop before the audience gets tired. Tell the audience that this is the most important topic you will cover.

Write the Time-Space percentage formula on the board or distribute copies of Handout 1 so the entire class can see it in writing. Seeing the formula in written form will make it easier for the audience to understand. If the audience is using copies of *The Basic Guide to Family Child Care Record Keeping* or the *Family Child Care Tax Workbook*, tell them that a complete explanation can be found in each book.

In explaining what hours may be claimed, first cover hours when children are present and then discuss hours when children are not present. List each area on the board (for example, "cleaning" and "cooking"). Use Handout 2 to help explain the hours that may be counted. Answer all questions in each subject area before moving to the next one.

Many providers have not claimed all the allowable business hours that they should. Encourage everyone to record and claim every hour that they use their home for business purposes. Tracking hours carefully for two different months of the year in order to calculate an average work week will probably be accepted by the IRS. Although it will seem to many to be a lot of work to keep track of these hours, stress how much this can raise their Time-Space percentage.

Commonly Asked Questions

May I count the hours I am shopping or driving children to school in my Time-Space percentage calculation?

No. You must be physically in your home. The Time-Space percentage calculation is a way of measuring how much of the home is used by your business. You may count the time playing outside in your yard.

May I count the outdoor yard space in my Time-Space percentage calculation?

No. Although an attached deck or porch is considered part of the home and should be included, a patio or the lawn and yard area should not be included.

What happens if I started my business in the middle of the year?

Calculate your Time-Space percentage for the months you were in business. For example, if you were in business August through December (22 weeks) and you worked an average of 11 hours a day, 5 days a week, your Time percentage would be 33 percent (1,210 work hours ÷ 3,696 total hours). Cross out the number printed on line 5 of **Form 8829** and enter 3,696. Calculate your Space percentage the same way, as if you had been in business for the entire year. Enter your house expenses for five months on column (b) in Part II of **Form 8829**.

What is a safe Time-Space percentage that the IRS won't challenge?

No one can predict what a particular IRS auditor will do. A provider who uses all her rooms regularly and works 10 hours a day, 52 weeks a year will have a Time-Space percentage of 30 percent. The vast majority of providers are probably claiming a Time-Space percentage between 30 percent and 40 percent. The overall average Time-Space percentage is likely to rise in light of IRS Revenue Ruling 92-3. Providers should not be shy about reporting a Time-Space percentage that is higher than average if they have the records to back up their percentage.

Teaching Family Child Care Record Keeping and Tax Preparation

Background Notes for the Trainer

The Time-Space percentage is the most common subject for IRS audits. It is likely that there will be more audits now because some tax preparers and providers are confused by how to fill out **Form 8829**.

In past years, some tax preparers and IRS auditors challenged the position that providers could claim hours spent using the home for business purposes when children were not present. This issue was settled with the issuance of Revenue Ruling 92-3. Providers are more likely to have trouble in audits when they do not have accurate records that show when they worked.

Providers should include the space in their garage in calculating the square footage of their home.

Providers should not assume that their tax preparer understands how to calculate the Time-Space percentage correctly. Tell providers to look closely at how the tax preparer has calculated this number. Providers need to be assertive in this area. Tell providers to give their tax preparer a copy of the handouts or copies of *The Basic Guide to Family Child Care Record Keeping* or the *Family Child Care Tax Workbook.*

If providers have underestimated their Time-Space percentage for an earlier year, they can file an amended tax return (**Form 1040X Amended U.S. Individual Tax Return**) going back three years. Providers should be careful in how they reconstruct their records of hours worked. They could use the current year of hours worked as a guide.

Some providers set up several rooms in their home to be used exclusively for their business. In 1993 the IRS issued a new clarification on this in the instructions to **Form 8829**. Providers must do two Time-Space percentage calculations, one for the exclusive-use room and one for the rest of the home. Providers should be encouraged to take advantage of this clarification.

Sometimes the provider's spouse is also operating a business out of the home and claiming a home office deduction. The space in the home must be allocated to each business. In this situation, the provider's Space percentage can never be 100 percent. Having two businesses in one home will not change the calculation of the provider's Time percentage.

The Time-Space Percentage

The Time-Space percentage is the single most important number to calculate for your business.

The Time-Space formula:

$$\frac{\text{\# hours home used in business}}{\text{Total \# hours in a year}} \quad \text{x} \quad \frac{\text{\# square feet of home used in business}}{\text{Total \# square feet in home}} \quad = \quad \text{Time-Space Percentage}$$

Use the Time-Space formula to allocate business use of shared business and personal expenses such as the following:

House repairs and maintenance

House depreciation

Rent

Property tax

Mortgage interest

Utilities

House insurance

Home improvements

Personal property depreciation: furniture and appliances (excluding such items as computer, TV, VCR, radio, tape recorder, and piano)

Land improvements

Household supplies and toys

Note:
Instead of using the Time-Space percentage, you may allocate business use for the above items by calculating actual business use, if you can document your calculation.

The Time Percentage: What Hours May Be Counted?

$$\frac{\text{\# hours home used in business}}{\text{Total \# hours in a year}} = \text{Time percentage}$$

Include in this calculation hours spent in your home:

- Caring for children, from when the first child arrives until the last child leaves.

- Cleaning up the house for the business before and after the children are present.

- Meal preparation for the children in care.

- Preparing activities for the children.

- Interviewing prospective parents.

- Talking to parents on the phone.

- Keeping business records and preparing taxes.

- Meal planning and preparing shopping lists for the business.

- Filling out paperwork for the Child Care Food Program.

Note:
You may not count time twice. For example, caring for children while engaged in a business activity described above.

You may not count hours spent away from home in activities such as shopping or transporting children to school.

© Redleaf National Institute, *Teaching Family Child Care Record Keeping and Tax Preparation:*
A Curriculum for Trainers (St. Paul: Redleaf Press, 1998), 1-800-423-8309.

The Time Percentage: How to Keep Records

- It is vital to have accurate records of the hours spent on your business throughout the year.

- Save your contract or other record that describes your normal workday hours.

- Use a calendar to track your business hours. For example:

S	M	T	W	T	F	S
1 business cleaning, 1hr prsnl cleaning,1hr bus cooking, 1 hr	2 7pm-business cleaning, 1hr	3 Juan leaves 5:10 10 min	4 4am-business cleaning, 1 hr 7pm-personal cleaning, 1 hr	5 7pm-cooking 30 min	6 7pm-business cleaning, 1 hr	7 plan trip to park, 30 min
8 prsnl cleaning,2 hr balance checkbook 30 min	9	10 talk to Claire's mother, 15 min	11	12 Mr. Taylor call 40 min	13 5-6 pm interview Smiths	14 plan menus, 1 hr
15 prsnl cleaning,2 hr call from Juan's father-Juan is ill, 20 min	16 business cleaning 1 hr	17	18 business cleaning 1 hr	19	20 business cleaning 1 hr	21 plan menus, 1 hr
22 prsnl cleaning 2 hr	23 Sharon leaves 5:30, 30 min	24 business cleaning 1 hr	25 Todd arrives 6:45, 15 min.	26 business cleaning 1 hr	27 Maria stays overnight, 5pm	28 parents pick-up Maria 9 am, 16 hrs

Provider's normal hours: 7 a.m. to 5 p.m.
Total extra hours: 32 hours, 40 minutes
Average per week: 8 hours, 10 minutes

- If you can't keep a daily record, prepare a weekly or monthly schedule and stick to it. For example:

S	M	T	W	T	F	S
	daily clean, 1 hr		cook, 1 hr			
	daily clean, 1 hr		cook, 1 hr			
	daily clean, 1 hr		cook, 1 hr			

The Space Percentage

$$\frac{\text{\# square feet of home used in business}}{\text{Total \# square feet in home}} \quad = \quad \text{Space percentage}$$

List each room in your home and measure the square feet in each room. If you use the room on a regular basis for your business, count the square feet as being used in business. For example:

Is area regularly used for business activities?		If yes, count as business space	If no, do not count as business space
Living room	Yes	250 sq. ft	
Dining room	Yes	150 sq. ft	
Kitchen	Yes	150 sq. ft	
Bathroom	Yes	100 sq. ft	
Entryway/stairs	Yes	150 sq. ft	
Second floor hallway	Yes	150 sq. ft	
Master bedroom	Yes	250 sq. ft	
Child's bedroom	No		150 sq. ft
Child's bedroom	No		150 sq. ft
Bathroom	Yes	100 sq. ft	
Basement laundry room	Yes	75 sq. ft	
Basement furnace area	Yes	50 sq. ft	
Basement storage area	Yes/No	175 sq. ft	200 sq. ft
Detached garage	Yes	400 sq. ft	
Total		2,000 sq. ft	500 sq. ft

$\frac{2,000}{2,500} = 80\%$ Space percentage

Note:
Many providers regularly use all the square feet in their home for business purposes. Their Space percentage would be 100 percent.

© Redleaf National Institute, *Teaching Family Child Care Record Keeping and Tax Preparation:*
A Curriculum for Trainers (St. Paul: Redleaf Press, 1998), 1-800-423-8309.

Exclusive-Use Rooms and the Time-Space Percentage

- Providers who use one or more rooms exclusively for child care should calculate a Time-Space percentage for both the exclusive-use room(s) and for the rest of the home and then add the percentages together.

- Exclusive use of a room means absolutely no personal use in the evenings or on weekends.

In the example below, lets assume the following:
2,000 square foot home
1,800 square feet used regularly for child care
200 square foot room used 100% for child care
30% Time percentage for nonexclusive space

STEP 1.
Calculate the Time-Space percentage of exclusive-use room.

$$\frac{200}{2,000} = 10\% \text{ Space percentage x 100\% Time percentage} = 10\% \text{ Time-Space percentage}$$

STEP 2.
Calculate Time-Space percentage of nonexclusive-use space.

$$\frac{1,800}{2,000} = 90\% \text{ Space percentage x 30\% Time percentage} = 27\% \text{ Time-Space percentage}$$

STEP 3.
Add two Time-Space percentages.

10% + 27% = 37% Time-Space percentage

Note:
If all the rooms in the home were used regularly for child care, the Time-Space percentage would be 30 percent (100% Space x 30% Time).

Unit C: Business Expenses

Introduction

This unit covers how to claim all business deductions except for helpers (see Unit D) and depreciation (see Unit E). The challenge of teaching providers what can be deducted as business expenses and how to deduct them is deciding which deductions you will talk about. No trainer can adequately cover all the allowable business deductions in one workshop. You must decide beforehand the key areas you will discuss. For a comprehensive list of business deductions, see *The Basic Guide to Family Child Care Record Keeping.* For a description of how to calculate the Time-Space percentage, see the IRS Revenue Ruling 92-3 and *The Basic Guide.* You may use the *Calendar-Keeper* to illustrate how to keep records of business deductions throughout the year. See the *Family Child Care Tax Workbook* for the latest information about vehicle depreciation.

Key Points to Cover

Providers, like all other businesses, are entitled to deduct all expenses that are both "ordinary and necessary" to operate their business. An ordinary expense is one that is "customary or usual" in the family child care business. A necessary expense is one that is "helpful and appropriate" in the conduct of the family child care business. An expense does not have to be indispensable to be considered necessary. The facts and circumstances of each case will determine whether a specific expense is ordinary and necessary. An expense may be deductible for one provider and not deductible for another. For example, a provider who uses her garden to teach her children about plants will be able to deduct part of the costs of her garden tools, but a provider who does not use her garden in her business may not deduct any of her garden expenses.

Providers who have applied for or are exempt from state child care regulations may claim the same deductions as those providers who have met these regulations. Providers who are in violation of state regulations may claim all the same business deductions as a regulated provider except for those deductions associated with the house. The point to make here is that even "illegal" providers can claim many business deductions. Providers who are exempt from licensing or regulation may claim all house expenses such as house insurance and utilities. Although most providers who come to workshops already have met state regulations, it is still useful to teach these points because the providers are likely to be talking later with other unregulated providers and they should be encouraged to pass on this information. (See Handout 1.)

Understanding how to claim business expenses can be made much easier if providers are taught to separate them into distinct categories (see Handout 2). Business expenses can be divided into three categories: direct expenses, house expenses, and capital expenditures. Direct expenses are all listed on **Schedule C**; house expenses on **Form 8829**; and capital expenditures on either **Form 4562** or **Form 8829**. Providers should be told to first identify each business expense by one of these categories and then look to the different rules affecting each category.

Direct expenses: Literally hundreds of expenses are deductible under this category. (See Handout 3 for a partial list.) Try not to explain in detail every expense item. Providers may be overwhelmed by the many different deductions. Some of the more important expenses to cover include food, vehicle expenses, program supplies, helpers, gifts, and household expenses.

Every item that falls into the direct expense category must be deducted using the following rules (see Handout 4):

1) If the item is used 100 percent for the business, you may deduct 100 percent of the expense for the business. (Make sure you stress that 100 percent means exactly 100 percent, not 99 percent.)

2) If the item is used 100 percent for personal purposes, you may not deduct any of the expense for the business.

3) If the item is used for both business and personal purposes, you may deduct a portion of the cost of the item for the business. Use either the Time-Space percentage or an actual business-use percent.

Deducting vehicle expenses is the one exception to the direct expense rules described above (see Handout 5). Use either the Standard Mileage Rate Method or the Actual Vehicle Expenses Method (see Handouts 6 and 7). The vast majority of providers use the Standard Mileage Rate Method. Providers who own a newer vehicle and use it a high percentage of the time for business are probably better off using the actual vehicle expenses method. Important points to stress about vehicle expenses are *(a)* the mileage of a trip can be deducted if it is "primarily" for business purposes and *(b)* providers may keep "sufficient written evidence" of business trips in many ways (for example, receipts, field trip permission forms, photos, or notations on a calendar).

House expense: Handout 8 lists all the house expenses that are to be reported on **Form 8829**. Providers must use their Time-Space percentage to allocate their mortgage loan interest and real estate taxes between their **Schedule C** (after transferring these expenses from **Form 8829**) and **Schedule A** (see Handout 9).

Capital expenditures: Handout 10 lists the different categories of capital expenditures. Providers should be told that these distinct categories each have their own depreciation rules. In a workshop on business expenses, time may only allow you to identify specific expenditures under each category. A complete explanation of how to teach depreciation can be found in Unit E.

Teaching Techniques

It is important not to get bogged down by spending too much time explaining any one area of business deductions. No workshop can adequately cover all allowable business deductions for providers. Keep a close eye on the time left in your workshop to make sure you will be able to cover all the topics on your agenda. It may be difficult to judge how much time it will take to discuss a particular deduction. Depending on how many questions the audience asks, the amount of time can vary greatly. For example, it may take ten minutes for you to address the topic of vehicle expenses, but with questions from the audience, the discussion may last as long as forty minutes. In order to limit the discussion, you may want to say, "I'll take two more questions on this topic and then we will have to move on." You can also remind the audience that in order to cover all the topics they want to hear about, you must end the questioning.

Many providers have a hard time understanding what expenses are reported on **Form 8829 Expenses for Business Use of Your Home** and what expenses go directly onto **Schedule C**. You can explain this easier if the audience looks at copies of both forms. You could distribute copies of the *Family Child Care Tax Workbook* and teach from it. You also could make copies of the two forms or show them on an overhead projector. Whichever method you use, point out that all expenses associated with the maintenance and improvement of the physical building belong on **Form 8829**. Expenses associated with items that providers take with them when they move from the house are called personal property and are claimed directly on **Schedule C**.

What can be misleading is that **Schedule C** has expense categories such as "mortgage interest," "rent," "repairs and maintenance," "taxes," and "utilities." Explain this using an example: House rental costs go on **Form 8829**, while rental of carpet cleaning equipment belongs on **Schedule C**. Repairs on the furnace go on **Form 8829**; repairs of personal property such as furniture repairs go on **Schedule C**. A service contract on a built-in appliance goes on **Form 8829**, a service contract on a free-standing appliance belongs on **Schedule C**. Note: The only time it makes a difference which form the expense is entered on is when the provider exceeds the limit of expenses on **Form 8829** and has to carry them over to the next year.

When explaining the concept of the actual business-use percentage in determining how much to claim as a business expense (for items used for both business and personal uses), be careful not to encourage providers to over-use this method. For example, if a provider is claiming an actual business-use percentage for a variety of items (such as paper towels, personal property depreciation, toys, all supplies, and laundry soap), *and* she is claiming the Time-Space percentage for all other shared expenses, the IRS may conclude that she is trying to work every angle too closely. If the IRS thinks that a provider is using the actual business-use percentage for all items that have a heavy business use, and the Time-Space percentage for all items having a light business use, they may ask the provider to calculate all expenses using the actual business-use method. Recommend that providers use the actual business-use percentage for larger items such as home improvements or expensive play equipment and for only a few smaller items such as paper towels. It only makes sense to use the actual business-use percentage if it is significantly greater than the Time-Space percentage.

You can end your workshop by asking the audience: "Based on your attendance at this workshop, what business deductions might you claim this year?" Allow the audience time to answer. They will usually come up with most of the items on this list: the fee for the class, the cost of any record-keeping or tax books purchased at the class, travel expenses to and from the class, helper's wage (if the helper is caring for the children), and the fact that the provider's cost for having someone provide her own children with child care may be counted toward her own child care tax credit. If the provider is staying overnight away from home to attend the work-shop, the provider may also deduct the cost of lodging and 50 percent of the cost of food eaten. Ending the class with this "pop quiz" offers participants a chance to share what they've learned and reinforces some of what was covered earlier. This technique will help you to close on a positive, affirmative note.

Commonly Asked Questions

When may I begin claiming expenses for my business?

As soon as you are ready and able to care for children and are telling others you are ready to care for children. If you begin advertising in March that you are ready to take children, and your first child isn't enrolled until June, you may claim all your business expenses starting in March. If you purchase items in anticipation of opening your business, before you are ready to care for children, you must amortize their cost over sixty months. (See the *Family Child Care Tax Workbook* for an explanation of start-up costs.)

May I claim the car mileage when I drive to the grocery store and buy food for my family and my business?

If this trip was made "primarily" for business purposes, you may claim all the mileage. If it was "primarily" for personal purposes, you may not claim any of the mileage. Evidence that you purchased more business food than personal food would probably make it "primarily" a business trip. You shouldn't claim every trip to the grocery store even if you always spend more on food for the business. The IRS will probably determine that you have made some personal trips. A safe way to deal with grocery trips is to claim every other trip. Do not try to claim a percentage of the mileage for the trips because this is not consistent with using the "primary" purpose test.

May I claim my monthly phone bill as a business expense?

The cost of the first phone line into a home is always considered personal and cannot be deducted as a business expense. A second phone line may be deducted, if it is used for business. Even a provider who did not have a phone but purchased one because local law required this cannot deduct the cost. (See Revenue Ruling 92-3 in the appendix.) Providers may deduct the cost of portable phones, answering machines, call forwarding, and call waiting as business expenses.

Why can't I claim all of my property tax and mortgage interest expenses on Schedule A?

Providers cannot choose to list all of these expenses on **Schedule A**. IRS law requires providers to split their expenses between **Schedule A** and **Form 8829**, according to the business use of the home. Most providers will use their Time-Space percentage as their business use. Providers are always better off claiming expenses on **Form 8829** than on **Schedule A** because their business income is taxed more heavily due to of Social Security taxes. Any expenses on **Form 8829** will reduce business income.

An IRS agent told me I couldn't deduct the cost of _____ because it's not an ordinary and necessary business expense. Is this correct?

Some IRS agents (and some tax preparers) do not understand the business of family child care. Family child care is a unique business that uses the home and most items in the home for business and personal purposes. Items such as toothpaste, birthday party expenses, garden tools, and plastic storage boxes are not normally thought of as business expenses, but these are ordinary and necessary expenses for many providers. Providers and tax preparers may have to spend time educating the IRS agent about the nature of the family child care business.

Background Notes for the Trainer

Providers are often confused about which category they should list their expenses on **Schedule C**. Are toys "supplies" or "other expenses"? Where do cable TV expenses and gifts belong? Providers won't be penalized for listing items on one line of **Schedule C** instead of another (with the exception of meals and entertainment that are subject to the 50 percent rule). It is good advice to spread expenses out by using the several lines under "other" expenses, rather than lumping many items under a specific line such as "supplies." A single large expense put on one line may trigger an audit. Providers and their tax preparers should set up a consistent way of grouping expenses. *The Basic Guide to Family Child Care Record Keeping* offers one method of categorizing business expenses on **Schedule C**. Providers may choose to set up their own method. As long as the provider has records showing which expenses were put on which lines, everything will be okay.

Many questions about what is deductible or how much of a particular expense is deductible are difficult to answer in a workshop. The situation is often not simple and the trainer does not know all of the facts surrounding the circumstances of the person asking the question. For this reason, many trainers tend to give more conservative answers to questions in class than when talking to providers individually, when they can learn more of the specific details surrounding the situation.

Some providers are very cautious about claiming expenses and others are very aggressive. To handle questions about what is deductible or how much of a particular expense is deductible, introduce the concept of the "conservative" and "assertive" approaches to claiming business expenses. For example, answer difficult questions such as "Can I deduct 100 percent of the cost of someone who comes into my home and cleans my rugs?" in the following manner: "If you are being conservative you can claim at least a portion of this expense, probably half of it, if the rugs are used in your business. If you take an assertive position and argue that the only reason you are having your rugs professionally cleaned is because of your business, then you should claim 100 percent of the expense."

Providers should be told that they must make their own decision about how much risk to take in filling out their tax forms. The more assertive a position a provider takes, the more careful the provider should be about keeping good records. Tax preparers and IRS agents can take different positions about what is deductible.

Commercial tax guides such as *Consumer Report's Guide to Income Tax* and *H&R Block Income Tax Guide* can help you better understand what expenses can be deducted for a child care business. These guides also provide good summaries of general tax principles.

Business Deductions for Regulated and Unregulated Providers

- To deduct expenses for their home, providers must have applied for, been granted, or be exempt from having a license, certification, registration or approval as a family or group child care home under their state laws.

- If providers do not meet mandatory state requirements, they may not claim any of the following house expenses as business deductions:

> Casualty losses
>
> Mortgage loan interest
>
> Real estate taxes
>
> House insurance
>
> House repairs and maintenance
>
> Utilities
>
> Rent
>
> House depreciation
>
> Home improvements

- Providers who do not meet a *voluntary* state regulation may still deduct all allowable house expenses.

- Providers who are in violation of state requirements may still claim all direct expenses and personal property depreciation as business expenses.

The Three Categories of Business Expenses

Direct Expenses are

- incurred for use by the business.

- usually claimed all in one year.

- often both business and personal expenses (for example, lightbulbs, paper towels, toilet paper). Providers may determine the business deduction by applying their Time-Space percentage or an actual business-use percent.

Note:
Do not use the Time-Space percentage on food expenses listed on **Schedule C.**

House Expenses are

- incurred for the purpose of maintaining or repairing your home.

- usually claimed all in one year.

- allocated between business and personal use by applying the Time-Space percentage in most situations.

- listed on **Form 8829.**

Capital Expenditures are

- those made to purchase, improve, or increase the value of property usually worth at least $100.

- usually spread over a number of years by using depreciation.

- allocated between business and personal use by applying the Time-Space percentage or an actual business-use percent.

- listed on **Form 4562** or **Form 8829.**

Examples of Direct Business Expenses

Advertising

Vehicle Expenses

Employee Wages, Taxes, and Benefits

Liability Insurance

Business Interest

Legal and Professional Services

Office Expenses

Bank Service Charges/Bounced Checks

Association Dues and Publications

Education/Training

Rent of Business Equipment

Supplies

Laundry and Cleaning

Gifts to Children and Their Parents

Meals and Business Entertainment Away from Home

Telephone Services (Call Forwarding, Answering Machine)

Food

Household Tools

Yard Tools

Toys and Games

Household Items

Claiming Direct Business Expenses

This example assumes a Time-Space percentage of 30 percent.

Expense	Cost	100% business expenses	Shared business and personal expenses	Business deduction
Fee for "Guiding Behavior" workshop	$15	Yes		$15
Wages for helpers	$856	Yes		$856
Crayons, supplies	$7.25	Yes		$7.25
Lightbulbs	$5.60		Yes	$5.60 x 30% = $1.68
Yard hose	$18.50		Yes	$18.50 x 30% = $5.55
Paper towels	$32.00		Yes	$32.00 x 75% actual business-use % = $24

Recording Vehicle Expenses

- Use either the Standard Mileage Rate Method ($0.325 per mile for 1998) or the Actual Vehicle Expenses Method.

- If a trip is "primarily" for business purposes, claim the entire trip for business.

- For grocery store trips to buy both business and personal food, claim all of the mileage if you purchase more business food than personal food.

- Providers need only keep "sufficient written evidence" of business trips. It is not necessary to keep a mileage log.

- Evidence of trips include notations on a calendar, receipts, canceled checks, photos, letters from parents, field trip permission forms, and admission tickets.

- For multiple trips to the same destination, record the mileage once and use the same number for all subsequent trips. For trips to destinations that you only travel to once or twice a year, record the mileage during the trip.

- You may claim the following as business expenses regardless of which method you use to claim vehicle expenses: parking fees, tolls, fares (bus, subway, train), a portion of interest on vehicle loans, and a portion of the state and local personal property taxes on the vehicle.

Using the Standard Mileage Rate Method to Claim Vehicle Expenses

STEP 1.
Regularly record the destinations of business trips on a calendar and list the mileage next to each trip.

STEP 2.
Multiply the number of trips to each destination by the mileage and total the result.

STEP 3.
Multiply the total by the standard mileage rate ($0.325 for 1998).

For example:

Al's Grocery Store	26 trips x 3 miles = 78 miles
First Bank	12 trips x 2 miles = 24 miles
Como Park	12 trips x 5 miles = 60 miles
Tots Toy Store	10 trips x 4 miles = 40 miles
Safeway Grocery Store	26 trips x 2 miles = 52 miles
Other trips (list)	1,621 miles
Total	1,875 miles

1,875 x .325 = $609.38 business mileage deduction

STEP 4.
Record the total on **Schedule C**, line 10. In addition, fill out Section B, Part V of **Form 4562 Depreciation and Amortization** or Part IV of **Schedule C**.

Note:
Providers may also claim a portion of the interest payments on their vehicle loan and a portion of any state and local personal property taxes on the vehicle. The business portion of these expenses is the percentage of total miles the vehicle is driven for business purposes.

Providers using this method may not claim expenses for vehicle insurance (even if purchased specifically for the business) or vehicle repairs (even if damage was caused while on a business trip).

Using the Actual Vehicle Expenses Method to Claim Vehicle Expenses

STEP 1.
Calculate your total business miles using the same method as described for the Standard Mileage Rate Method.

STEP 2.
Divide the number of business miles driven by the total number of miles driven.

$$\frac{1,875 \text{ business miles}}{12,875 \text{ total miles}} = 15\%$$

STEP 3.
List the actual expenses for maintaining your vehicle and multiply by your business-use percent.

Gasoline	$120
Oil	20
Repairs	205
Insurance	500
Taxes and license	100
Vehicle loan interest	250
Total	$1,195 x 15% = $179.25

Note:
You may also take expenses for the depreciation of your vehicle under the following conditions.

- If the business use of the vehicle is 50 percent or less, depreciate the vehicle using 5-year straight-line rules.

- If the business use of the vehicle is more than 50 percent, claim depreciation using either 5-year straight-line rules, 5-year 200 percent declining balance, or Section 179 rules.

List of House Expenses

Casualty Losses

Mortgage Loan Interest

Real Estate Taxes

House Insurance

House Repairs and Maintenance (for example, furnace repair or cleaning, service contracts on appliances, and broken window repair)

Utilities (gas, electric, water, sewer, garbage)

House Rent

Claiming House Expenses

This example assumes a Time-Space percentage of 30 percent.

	Total Yearly Expense	Form 8829 Business Expense	Schedule A Personal Expense
	100%	30%	70%
Mortgage Loan Interest	$3,000	$900	$2,100
Real Estate Taxes	$4,000	$1,200	$2,800

The personal expense portion of mortgage loan interest and real estate taxes may be claimed as an itemized personal deduction on **Schedule A.**

Examples of Business Capital Expenditures

Vehicle

Home Improvements
(for example, remodeling, new roof, wall-to-wall carpeting)

House

Land Improvements
(for example, fence, landscaping, new driveway)

Personal Computer

Entertainment/Recreation or Amusement Items
(for example, TV, VCR, record player)

Other Personal Property
(for example, appliances, furniture, play equipment, lawn mower, snowblower)

Unit D: Hiring Helpers

Introduction

This unit covers how to distinguish an independent contractor from an employee and the tax consequences of both.

The most important message to communicate to providers on the subject of assistants is that, in most cases, they should be treating assistants as employees. This is a complex subject and one that does not affect the majority of providers. For a summary of the subject, see *The Basic Guide to Family Child Care Record Keeping*. For an example of how the employer-employee forms are to be filled out, see the latest *Family Child Care Tax Workbook*.

Key Points to Cover

The single most important message to communicate on this subject is that providers who hire people to help them care for the children in family child care should treat these helpers as employees. Although there are several exceptions to this rule, the vast majority of helpers working for family child care providers are employees.

Many providers treat their helpers as independent contractors and do not withhold any employment taxes or file any tax forms on their helpers. Providers who do this are taking a risk because, if audited, they will be required to pay the total Social Security taxes owed for each employee, plus interest, along with any possible penalties. (See Handout 1.)

The IRS requires providers to fill out a number of tax forms for their employees (see Handout 2). Although the prospect of filling out these forms can seem overwhelming to many providers, they should be made aware that these forms are meant to be used by providers. Some states have additional state tax forms that are required. If you are familiar with these state rules, summarize them as well.

If a provider is using an independent contractor and pays any one person $600 or more in a year, the provider must file a **Form 1099 Miscellaneous Income** with the IRS after the end of the year. This form gives the IRS the opportunity to find out if a person who earned at least $600 in a year reported this money to the IRS as income.

There is a slight tax saving if providers hire their own spouse, and there are significant tax savings if providers hire their own children who are younger than 18 years old. Young children will not have to pay Social Security taxes or federal unemployment taxes and, in most cases, they will not owe income taxes. Providers are always entitled to deduct such wages as a business expense. (See Handout 3.)

Teaching Techniques

The topic of hiring assistants can be a complex and frustrating subject for many providers. Before discussing the subject, you may want to ask the audience, "How many of you pay someone any amount of money to help care for your children in child care, not including your own family members?" If only a few raise their hands, you may consider not taking time with the entire group to cover this subject. Ask the one or two people to stay after the workshop or talk to them at the break about handling employees.

Providers who treat their assistants as independent contractors are often shocked to hear that they have employees and of the extensive IRS reporting requirements. Realize that many in the workshop will treat you as the bearer of bad news. Some providers may be upset and angry. Some providers may also report that their tax preparer or another trainer told them they could treat assistants as independent contractors. Present the rules about employees in a firm manner. No provider should leave any workshop on this topic without understanding clearly that the IRS considers assistants as employees.

You can illustrate the difference between an employee and an independent contractor by using the example of a plumber and an assistant found in the *Family Child Care Tax Workbook*. Make it clear that there is no doubt that the IRS will consider helpers as employees.

Ask the members of the audience to tell you how many hours a week an assistant is working for them. This will give you the opportunity to reinforce the message about treating assistants as employees. If a provider says her assistant works ten or more hours a week, you can be very direct in saying that this assistant is an employee and that the provider could owe a lot in back taxes and interest if she doesn't file the proper forms. If the provider says her assistant works only a few hours a year, you should say that the assistant is still an employee, but the consequences for not withholding employment taxes properly are not as serious. It is more important to get the message across to those with full-time assistants than to those who use helpers only occasionally.

It is not a good idea to explain the details of filling out the tax forms required when using assistants. While these forms can be confusing, and the amount of forms may frighten many providers, you would need at least a half hour to adequately discuss the subject. Rather than focussing on the specifics of these forms and how to do withholding, a workshop covering the subject of assistants should focus on the idea that providers have employees, not independent contractors. Recommend that providers with assistants either use a payroll service or seek the assistance of a qualified tax preparer to help them fill out all of the IRS forms properly.

Commonly Asked Questions

Should I hire my spouse to help me in my business?

A provider should treat a spouse like any other employee when filling out all necessary federal and state tax forms. Any money the spouse earns must be reported as income. The provider will save some money by deducting the employer share of Social Security and Medicare as a business expense. There are greater tax savings if the provider offers medical insurance as an employee benefit to the spouse. Such insurance could cover the provider and the provider's children. (See the *Family Child Care Tax Workbook.*)

Can I hire my own 8-year-old child, even if my licensing worker says that substitutes must be at least 16 years old?

Some states have laws setting the minimum age for substitutes or helpers to remain in compliance with child/staff ratios. These rules have nothing to do with providers who hire their own children but who aren't using them to meet local child/staff ratio requirements. Such providers may hire their own children at a very young age to do simple tasks such as picking up toys, cleaning, and setting the table for lunch.

Isn't it true that I don't have to treat my assistant as an employee as long as I pay them less than $600 in a year?

No. Many providers are confused about the $600 limit for **Form 1099**. There is no minimum amount that allows you to treat someone as an independent contractor rather than an employee. If you do have an independent contractor and pay her less than $600 a year, you don't have to file a **Form 1099**. If this person is actually an employee, you must still treat them as an employee, regardless of how little you pay them.

Should I pay my own child with a check for working for my business?

The important point is to have good records that show that the child was paid for work and not just given the money as an allowance. Prepare receipts that detail what work was done and how much was paid. Payment by check from a business checkbook is further evidence of a business expense, but it is not required. If payments are made in cash, there should be some written record of the transaction.

Background Notes for the Trainer

Providers are usually not happy to hear about the many forms to fill out and taxes to be paid for hiring assistants. You may want to point out that if assistants are being paid only a few hundred dollars a year, the taxes owed are very small. Some providers may choose to ignore the reporting requirements and take the risk of being caught in an audit. But if audited, the taxes and interest (and perhaps the penalties) are not much on a few hundred dollars. Although this may be presented as an alternative, be careful to make sure that providers understand that the law requires them to file the proper tax forms for assistants.

Some bookkeeping services will provide assistance to employers who have only one employee. These services will file all the necessary forms and even write checks for the employee after deducting the proper withholding amounts. You may want to investigate whether bookkeeping services in your area will help small child care businesses. Check in the local phone book or ask the local Chamber of Commerce for the names of bookkeepers. Their fees are usually reasonable. One national company that provides this service is Automated Data Processing (ADP). You should also refer providers to local tax preparers who have experience in this area. They can help get providers off on the right foot with hired employees (and when providers' hire their own children) by initially setting up the reporting system.

There are other potential tax benefits if providers hire their spouses to work for their business. Providers can set up a benefit plan to cover health insurance (for the spouse and their own children), retirement, dental, and other services. The cost of such plans are fully deductible as a business expense. Most providers are not in a position to pay enough money to a spouse to make such benefit plans feasible, but some are. You may want to alert the few providers who are in this situation that they should ask their tax preparer or a benefits consultant for further information.

Watch out for a "catch-22" situation in the issue of independent contractor versus employee. If a provider treats her assistant as an independent contractor and the assistant earns more than $600 a year, she must file a **Form 1099**. Failing to file this form will result in penalties to the provider. However, **Form 1099** can be used as a trap to catch providers who really have employees but are considering them as independent contractors in order to avoid paying employment taxes. The IRS watches for individuals who receive only one **Form 1099** at the end of the year. They may ask this person to prove they are not an employee of the provider since they apparently aren't working for anyone else. The solution? Do not treat assistants as independent contractors; report them as employees. Providers who are trying to hide their employees from the IRS may be better off not filing **Form 1099** at all to avoid the attention this form brings.

Teaching Family Child Care Record Keeping and Tax Preparation

Employee versus Independent Contractor

- Providers who hire people to help them care for children should treat these assistants as employees.

There are several exceptions to this rule:

- If the assistant is hired through an agency and the provider pays the agency for the service.

- If the assistant works for other providers and is clearly in the business of providing substitute care.

- If the assistant is offering a "special service" (for example, a puppet show or ballet class).

- Providers are required to treat assistants as employees even if they are providing help for only a few hours a month.

- The IRS is taking a strict stand about treating assistants as employees and not as independent contractors.

Requirements for Hiring an Employee

The following tax forms must be filed if you have an employee:

- Verification of eligibility to work in the United States (**Form I-9**)

- Employer Identification Number (**Form SS-4**)

- Federal income tax withholding (**Form W-4**)

- Quarterly Social Security and Medicare withholding (**Form 941**)

- Federal unemployment withholding (**Form 940**)

- End of the year reporting of wages and withholding (**Form W-2** and **W-3**)

Employees must be paid at least the minimum wage ($5.15 per hour in 1998). There is a special exception for providers who hire only one employee in a year (see the *Family Child Care Tax Workbook*). In addition, state laws may require employers to pay workers' compensation and withhold state income and unemployment taxes.

Hiring Family Members

- Providers should treat family members who work for their business as employees.

- There is a slight tax benefit to hiring your spouse because the employer share of Social Security and Medicare is deductible as a business expense.

- If you pay your own child who is 18 years old or over, the child must report the income as wages and pay Social Security. Wages are not subject to federal unemployment tax up to age 21.

- If you pay your own child who is under age 18, the child does not have to pay Social Security or Medicare.

- If you hire your own child, make sure the work is related to business, the pay is reasonable (what another child of the same age would receive), and the pay is distinguished from a personal allowance.

© Redleaf National Institute, *Teaching Family Child Care Record Keeping and Tax Preparation:*
A Curriculum for Trainers (St. Paul: Redleaf Press, 1998), 1-800-423-8309.

Unit E: Depreciation

Introduction

This unit covers the various rules of depreciation that affect family child care providers. The subject of depreciation is probably the most difficult topic to teach to family child care providers. In order to present the subject in a clear and organized manner, allow plenty of time for preparation. For a summary of how to identify the different categories of depreciation expenses and how to keep records for them, see *The Basic Guide to Family Child Care Record Keeping*. For a discussion of how to apply the current depreciation rules to each category of business expense, see the *Family Child Care Tax Workbook*.

Key Points to Cover

Items that are used for business purposes and last longer than a year should be expensed over several years, under the rules of depreciation. As a general rule of thumb, the IRS will allow taxpayers to expense in one year items that cost less than $100. Items that must be depreciated fall into one of seven distinct categories, and each category has its own depreciation rules (see Handout 1). For a complete description of each category, see *The Basic Guide to Family Child Care Record Keeping.*

Personal Computer: Many providers use a personal computer in their business for record keeping or for children's games. Providers may depreciate their computer based on the actual business-use percentage, not their Time-Space percentage (see Handout 2). It is necessary to keep some records of how much time the computer is used for business and personal purposes. Enter this expense on **Form 4562**, Part V.

Entertainment and Recreation Property: Items such as a TV, VCR, record and cassette player, and musical instruments must be depreciated under this category. Providers must use an actual business-use percentage and keep records in the same way as they would for a personal computer (see Handout 3). Enter these expenses on **Form 4562**, Part V.

Other Personal Property: All other personal property—such as furniture, appliances, and large play equipment—must be depreciated using the Time-Space percentage or the actual business-use percent method (see Handout 4). Enter this percent on **Form 4562**, Part II or Part III.

Home: Depreciating the home is an important source of business deductions (see Handout 5). Use the Time-Space percentage and enter the expense on **Form 8829**. Fundamental principles that should always be covered when discussing the home are *(a)* providers are always better off financially by depreciating their home; they should not listen to a tax preparer that tells them differently and *(b)* providers should be aware that if they sell their home, they may have to pay tax that year on the business portion of any profit in the sale of the home.

Sale of Home: There have been significant changes in the rules for providers who sell their home after May 6, 1997. You should strongly urge providers who are considering selling their home to seek professional tax help up to three years before they decide to sell. (See Handout 6.)

Home Improvements: New additions, remodeling, and a new furnace are examples of home improvements. Use the Time-Space percentage or actual business-use percent and enter the expense on **Form 8829**. (See Handout 7.)

Land Improvements: Land improvements are those items that are attached to the land and increase its value, such as a fence, patio, and landscaping. Use the Time-Space percentage or actual business-use percent and enter the expense on **Form 4562**. (See Handout 8.)

Vehicle: Providers may only depreciate their vehicle if they choose to use the Actual Vehicle Expenses Method of calculating vehicle expenses and not the Standard Mileage Rate Method. Use the actual business-use percent and enter the expense on **Form 4562**, Part V.

Keeping track of depreciation expenses over the years can become complex. It is important to keep careful records of what depreciation rules are in effect each year. Providers must also depreciate expenses for each year separately. (See Handouts 9, 10, and 11.)

Deducting Unclaimed Depreciation: Providers who have not previously claimed depreciation can file **Form 3115** and deduct it in the current tax year (see Handout 12). This new rule can significantly benefit many providers because many have not claimed all of the depreciation they were entitled to on their furniture, appliances, television, home improvements, and home. The rule allows providers to go back more than three years to pick up unclaimed depreciation for as long as the provider was in business and still owns the property. (See the *Family Child Care Tax Workbook.*)

Teaching Techniques

The depreciation rules can be difficult for an audience to follow. Because it is easy to confuse providers with the unfamiliar concepts of "accelerated" or "straight-line" depreciation and Section 179 rules, proceed slowly with this topic. Focus on how to identify in which category an item to be depreciated belongs rather than spending a lot of time on the details of how to apply a specific depreciation rule.

Here are some simple definitions of depreciable property:

*   Personal property—items that are not attached to the home or land that providers take with them when moving from their home.

*   Home improvements—items that are attached to the home and increase its value.

*   Land improvements—items that are attached to land and increase its value.

In a three-hour workshop on taxes, you do not need to go into much detail showing how to use the current rules to depreciate an item. Often providers are frustrated at the number of different depreciation rules. Because providers use their tax preparers to calculate depreciation, make sure providers understand that they are entitled to depreciate many different items. As a result, they should conduct an inventory of items used for their business. It is only with advanced workshops that you can explain depreciation rules at length.

When explaining depreciation, use a blackboard or flip chart as much as possible to illustrate practical examples:

$1500 computer
x 25% business use
$375 business basis
x 10% 1st year of 5-year straight-line
$37.50 depreciation claimed in year 1

Another example:

$1,000 play equipment purchased

If Time-Space percentage or business-use percent is less than 50%	If business-use percent is 50% or more
	Method #1
$1,000	$1,000
x 30% Time-Space percentage	x 80% business-use percent
$300	$800
x 7.14% 1st year of 7-year straight-line	x 7.14% 1st year of 7-year straight-line
$21.42 depreciation claimed in year 1	$57.12
	Method #2
	$1,000
	x 80% business-use percent
	$800 claim all in 1st year under Section 179 rules

Most providers are not going to keep a daily log tracking the business use of their computer, TV, VCR, and other entertainment and recreational property. Instead, encourage providers to keep a log for a few weeks at different times of the year to estimate business use. Put an example on the board to show that the provider is comparing hours of business use to hours of personal use, not to a twenty-four hour day. Here is an example of the use of a computer:

$$\frac{10 \text{ hours a week average business use}}{40 \text{ hours a week average total use}} = 25\% \text{ business use}$$

To illustrate what kinds of household items can be depreciated, identify a series of specific items in several rooms. For the living room, for example, name the sofa, chairs, end tables, lamp, and rug. (See *The Basic Guide to Family Child Care Record Keeping* for an explanation of the conservative and assertive approaches to identifying personal property for depreciation.) By identifying specific items, you will help providers understand that they may have hundreds of items that they can depreciate.

Too many tax preparers are still telling providers they shouldn't depreciate their home. You must firmly state that it is always the right thing to do. Point out that IRS **Publication 551 Basis of Assets** says that if a provider is entitled to claim depreciation, the IRS will treat the provider as if she did claim it. Because so much bad advice has been given out about home depreciation, ask the audience if they understand this point.

Every workshop usually contains providers who are in their first year of business and those who have many years of experience but have not depreciated their personal property. Trying to explain the depreciation rules to providers in these different situations can be made easier by clearly categorizing expenses. You may want to put these categories on the board:

1) Items costing less than $100: Claim in the year purchased.

2) Items costing more than $100: Depreciate over a number of years using depreciation rules. Exceptions to this are *(a)* personal property used more than 50 percent in the business under Section 179 rules and *(b)* repairs.

3) Items purchased before the business began (no matter what the original cost): Depreciate over a number of years using depreciation rules.

Commonly Asked Questions

Can I use my Time-Space percentage to calculate the business use of my TV and VCR?

No. Providers must calculate an actual business-use percent by keeping some records of the number of hours these items were used for business and personal purposes. Some tax preparers and IRS officials don't realize that entertainment and recreation items must be treated differently than other personal property, or they choose to ignore it.

May I begin depreciating my refrigerator this year, even though I began using it for my business several years ago?

Yes, but the provider will lose the depreciation deduction for the previous years unless she files an amended tax return. Providers need to understand that the clock starts ticking the year that any item is first used for business purposes and that the item must always be depreciated under the rules that were in effect for that first year. You may want to illustrate this point by writing on the board:

1996	1997	1998	1999	2000
Purchase refrigerator and first use for business. See 7-year straight-line rules.				
year 1 of 7-year straight-line	year 2	year 3	year 4	year 5

My new deck won't last 39 years. Why can't I depreciate it faster?

Home improvements must be depreciated over 39 years, regardless of the length of a loan or the estimated life of the item. If the deck wears out before the end of the depreciation period, the provider can claim all the remaining depreciation in the year the item is worn out. This point is important to stress, because many home improvements and personal property do not last the full depreciation period.

My husband and I built our home. Can we depreciate our home based on its fair market value when it was completed?

No. Providers may only depreciate the actual cost of materials and contractor fees. Sweat labor by husband and wife cannot be counted in determining the value of the house.

Is there anything I can do to reduce my taxes in the year I sell my home and transfer my business to my new home?

Yes. Providers who cannot avoid paying tax on the business portion of the profit on the sale of their home should attempt to lower their Time-Space percentage by working fewer hours or using fewer rooms. Providers may also want to check out doing a "like-kind exchange" to significantly reduce their tax liability.

What happens if I sell my home at a loss?

A declining housing market or making many home improvements over the years can create a loss in the sale of a home. Providers can claim their Time-Space percentage of such a loss as a deduction to their income in the year of sale. Therefore, it is preferable to be in business if the home is sold at a loss.

My basement is used exclusively for my business. How do I depreciate the items I purchase for this area?

Anything purchased for such a room may be claimed as a 100 percent business expense. Personal property may either be depreciated under regular depreciation rules or be taken as an expense in one year under Section 179 rules.

Should I depreciate my vehicle or claim the standard mileage rate?

The answer depends upon how often the vehicle is driven for business purposes and the value of the vehicle. If a vehicle is only a couple of years old and the provider drives the vehicle more than a third of the time for business, she may be better off using the Actual Vehicle Expense Method. Providers should calculate their vehicle expenses using both methods and use whichever method gives them a higher deduction. Providers can only use the Standard Mileage Rate Method if they choose to do so in the first year the vehicle is used for their business. If providers choose the Actual Vehicle Expenses Method in the first year the vehicle is used for their business, they cannot switch back to using the Standard Mileage Rate Method in later years.

Background Notes for the Trainer

The IRS has been looking closely at self-employed taxpayers who use computers for their business. Providers should be advised to keep records that track business and personal use. The higher the number of hours of business use, the more complete the record keeping that should be done.

Although providers may want to use accelerated depreciation rules, including Section 179, it is best to talk about using straight-line rules in a workshop. Straight-line rules are the simplest to explain. Providers should be warned about the possible negative consequences of using Section 179 rules. Providers who intend to go out of business within a couple of years should be aware of recapture rules. It is not a good idea to discuss recapture rules in a class, however, because the recapture rules are too confusing to most providers.

Often providers will complain at a workshop that their tax preparer told them not to depreciate their home or personal property. Encourage providers to start depreciating these items for the current year and file amended tax returns when possible. The IRS will depreciate a home even if the provider did not. Sometimes the workshop will turn into a general discussion of how to find competent tax preparers. Be prepared to give some pointers on how to work with tax preparers. (See *The Basic Guide to Family Child Care Record Keeping.*)

1998 Depreciation Rules for Capital Expenditures

DEPRECIATION CATEGORIES	RULES FOR DEPRECIATION
PERSONAL COMPUTER	
Business use 50% or less:	5-year straight-line
Business use more than 50%:	5-year straight-line, 5-year 200% declining balance, or Section 179
ENTERTAINMENT AND RECREATION PROPERTY	
(TV, VCR, cassette player)	
Business use 50% or less:	7-year straight-line
Business use more than 50%:	7-year straight-line, 7-year 200% declining balance, or Section 179
OTHER PERSONAL PROPERTY	
(Furniture, appliances, equipment)	
Time-Space percentage or business use 50% or less:	7-year straight-line, or 7-year 200% declining balance
Time-Space percentage or business use more than 50%:	7-year straight-line, 7-year 200% declining balance, or Section 179
HOUSE	
For all Time-Space percentages:	39-year straight-line
HOME IMPROVEMENT	
For all Time-Space or business-use percentages:	39-year straight-line
LAND IMPROVEMENT	
For all Time-Space or business-use percentages:	15-year straight-line or 150% declining balance
VEHICLE	
Business use 50% or less:	5-year straight-line
Business use more than 50%:	5-year straight-line, or 5-year 200% declining balance

Depreciating a Personal Computer

STEP 1.
Use the actual business-use percent, not the Time-Space percentage.

- If the business-use percent is 50% or less, use 5-year straight-line depreciation:

  Year 1   10%   Year 4   20%

  Year 2   20%   Year 5   20%

  Year 3   20%   Year 6   10%

  $1,500 computer x 25% business-use percent = $375 business basis
  $375 x 10% (year 1) = $37.50

- If the business-use percent is more than 50%, you have three choices:

  1)   5-year straight-line

  2)   5-year 200% declining balance

  3)   100% under Section 179

  Under Section 179:

  $1,500 computer x 70% business-use percent = $1,050 deduction in year 1

STEP 2.
Put personal computer depreciation on **Form 4562.**

Depreciating Entertainment and Recreation Property

STEP 1.
Use the actual business-use percent, not the Time-Space percentage.

- If the business-use percent is 50% or less, use 7-year straight-line depreciation:

Year 1	7.14%	Year 5	14.29%
Year 2	14.29%	Year 6	14.28%
Year 3	14.29%	Year 7	14.29%
Year 4	14.28%	Year 8	7.14%

$600 television x 40% business-use percent = $240 business basis
$240 x 7.14% (year 1) = $17.14

- If the business-use percent is more than 50%, you have three choices:

  1) 7-year straight-line

  2) 7-year 200% declining balance

  3) 100% under Section 179

  Under Section 179:

  $600 television x 60% business-use percent = $360 deduction in year 1

STEP 2.
Put entertainment and recreation depreciation on **Form 4562.**

Depreciating Other Personal Property

STEP 1.
Use either the Time-Space percentage or the actual business-use percent.

- If the Time-Space percentage or actual business-use percent is 50 percent or less, use 7-year straight-line depreciation:

  Year 1   7.14%   Year 5   14.29%

  Year 2   14.29%   Year 6   14.28%

  Year 3   14.29%   Year 7   14.29%

  Year 4   14.28%   Year 8   7.14%

  $1,000 (appliances) x 30% Time-Space percentage = $300 business basis
  $300 x 7.14% (year 1) = $21.42

  Note:
  Provider may also use 7-year 200% declining balance method.

- If the Time-Space percentage or actual business-use percent is more than 50%, you have three choices:

  1) 7-year straight-line

  2) 7-year 200% declining balance

  3) 100% under Section 179

  Under Section 179:

  $1,000 (appliances) x 75% business-use percent = $750 deduction in year 1

STEP 2.
Put other personal property depreciation on **Form 4562.**

Depreciating the Home

STEP 1.
Use the Time-Space percentage.

STEP 2.
Determine the home's adjusted basis.

Purchase price of home:	$150,000
Subtract value of land at time of purchase:	-$15,000
	$135,000

Add value of home improvements before child care business began:	+$3,500
adjusted basis	$138,500

STEP 3.
Multiply the home's adjusted basis by the Time-Space percentage.

$138,500 x 30% Time-Space percentage = $41,550 business basis

STEP 4.
Use 39-year straight-line depreciation for a home that is put into business use after May 13, 1993.

STEP 5.
Determine the depreciation percentage. For the first year, use the percentage from the IRS tables for the month the home was first used for business.

$41,550 x 2.461% (January) = $1,022.55

STEP 6.
For years 2–39, the depreciation percentage is 2.564%.

STEP 7.
Put home depreciation on **Form 8829.**

The Tax Consequences of Selling Your Home

There are new IRS rules for providers who sell their home after May 6, 1997. First, providers must pay capital gains tax on the business portion of the gain on the sale of the home if they have used the home for their business more than 36 months of the last 60 months before the home is sold. If this is the case, providers must also pay capital gains tax on the depreciation they claimed (or were entitled to claim) since they began using their home for business.

In order to meet this rule, providers can count days rather than months. In other words, a provider can avoid the capital gains tax if she has not used her home for business for 730 days (24 months = 730 days) in the last five years before the sale. A provider who is closed Saturday and Sunday for five years can count 520 days of personal use. When a provider adds up vacations, holidays, sick days, and other personal days, she may only have to close her business for a few months before selling it to meet the 24-month rule.

Second, when they sell their home providers must pay capital gains tax on any depreciation they claim (or are entitled to claim) after May 6, 1997. This is true regardless of whether the provider was in business for more than 36 months of the last 60 months before they sold their home.

There are two basic guidelines that providers who own a house should follow:

1) Providers are always better off financially by claiming depreciation deductions on their home if they are entitled to. IRS rules say that when providers sell their homes they will be treated as if they depreciated their home even if they didn't. In other words, providers will have to pay capital gains tax on their depreciation even if they did not claim the depreciation deduction.

2) Providers who are thinking about selling their home within the next three years should consult a professional tax preparer who can help them plan ahead to possibly reduce the tax consequences.

Here are some strategies to consider when selling your home:

Sell home at a large gain

a) Do not use your home for business for at least 24 months (730 days) out of the last 60 months before the sale. Providers may count days they did not work (weekends, holidays, and vacation) during these years.

b) Reduce your Time-Space percentage in the years leading up to the sale.

c) Conduct a like-kind exchange.

Sell home at a small gain

a) Pay the taxes on the gain and the depreciation.

b) Reduce your Time-Space percentage in the years leading up to the sale.

Sell home at a small or large loss

a) Do use your home for business for at least 36 months out of the last 60 months before the sale.

b) Increase your Time-Space percentage in the year of the sale.

Depreciating Home Improvements

STEP 1.
Use either the Time-Space percentage or the actual business-use percent.
Use 39-year straight-line depreciation for improvements after May 13, 1993.

STEP 2.
For the first year, use the percentage from the IRS tables for the month the home improvement was completed.

$5,000 new roof x 30% Time-Space percentage = $1,500
$1,500 x 1.391% (June) = $20.87

STEP 3.
For years 2–39, the depreciation percentage is 2.564%.

STEP 4.
Put major home improvement depreciation on **Form 8829.**

© Redleaf National Institute, *Teaching Family Child Care Record Keeping and Tax Preparation: A Curriculum for Trainers* (St. Paul: Redleaf Press, 1998), 1-800-423-8309.

Depreciating Land Improvements

STEP 1.
Use the Time-Space percentage or actual business-use percent.

STEP 2.
Use 15-year straight-line depreciation or 15-year 150 percent declining balance for 1998 expenses.

	Straight Line	150% declining balance		Straight Line	150% declining balance
Year 1	3.33%	5.00%	Year 9	6.67%	5.91%
Year 2	6.67%	9.50%	Year 10	6.66%	5.90%
Year 3	6.67%	8.55%	Year 11	6.67%	5.91%
Year 4	6.67%	7.70%	Year 12	6.66%	5.90%
Year 5	6.67%	6.93%	Year 13	6.67%	5.91%
Year 6	6.67%	6.23%	Year 14	6.66%	5.90%
Year 7	6.67%	5.90%	Year 15	6.67%	5.91%
Year 8	6.66%	5.90%	Year 16	3.33%	2.95%

$3,000 new fence x 25% Time-Space percentage = $750
$750 x 3.33% (year 1 straight-line) = $24.98
$750 x 5.00% (year 1 150% declining balance) = $37.50

STEP 3.
Put land improvement depreciation on **Form 4562.**

Amending the Tax Return

- Providers may go back three years to amend their tax returns and claim refunds.

- Providers must use depreciation rules in effect for the first year the item is put into business use.

Example: A provider had $4,000 worth of personal property when she started her business in 1994, but she did not depreciate it. In 1998 she files an amended return for the earlier years:

1994: No amended return may be filed.

1995: $4,000 x 27% Time-Space percentage = $1,080
$1,080 x 14.29% (year 2, 7-year straight-line) = $154.33
Reduce business taxable income in 1995 by $154.33

1996: $4,000 x 29% Time-Space percentage = $1,160
$1,160 x 14.29% (year 3, 7-year straight-line) = $165.76
Reduce business taxable income in 1996 by $165.76

1997: $4,000 x 28% Time-Space percentage = $1,120
$1,120 x 14.28% (year 4, 7-year straight-line) = $159.94
Reduce business taxable income in 1997 by $159.94

In 1998, provider claims depreciation amount for year 5 of 7-year straight-line.
$4,000 x 28% Time-Space percentage = $1,120
$1,120 x 14.29% = $160.05

- Use **Form 1040X** to file amended return.

Keeping Track of Depreciation Over the Years

The following chart shows how to keep records over the years for items depreciated in 1998 under 7-year 200 percent declining balance rules. After 1998 the depreciation rules may change. In this example we are assuming the depreciation rules remain the same for 1998–2001.

1998	1999	2000	2001
7-year 200%	7-year 200%	7-year 200%	7-year 200%
Year 1 stove	Year 2 stove	Year 3 stove	Year 4 stove
$800 x 25% = $200 x 14.29% = $28.58 **Total: $28.58**	$800 x 25% = $200 x 24.49% = $48.98	$800 x 25% = $200 x 17.49% = $34.98	$800 x 30% = $240 x 12.49% = $29.98
	Year 1 swing set	Year 2 swing set	Year 3 swing set
	$1,000 x 25% = $250 x 24.49% = $61.23 **Total $84.71**	$1,000 x 30% = $300 x 17.49% = $52.47	$1,000 x 30% = $300 x 17.49% = $52.47
		Year 1 clothes dryer	Year 2 clothes dryer
		$500 x 30% = $150 x 24.49% = $36.74 **Total $114.07**	$500 x 30% = $150 x 24.49% = $36.74
			Year 1 sofa
			$700 x 30% = $210 x 14.29% = $30.01 **Total $149.20**

Depreciation Worksheet

Description of Property	Put into Business Use (Month/Year)	Price*	Business-Use Percent**	Business Cost Basis***
House				
Home improvements				
Land improvements				
Personal computer				
Entertainment, recreation, and amusement items				
All other personal property items				

* Price: For all expenditures except the house, list the fair market value at the time of purchase or the purchase price, whichever is lower. To arrive at the price of the house, take the purchase price minus the value of the land at the time of purchase. Add to this the cost of any major home improvements made before your home was used by your business.

** Business-Use Percent: For the house, home improvements, land improvements, and other personal property, use your Time-Space percentage or an actual business-use percent. For a personal computer and entertainment items, use an actual business-use percent, not your Time-Space percentage.

*** Business Cost Basis: Multiply the Price for each item by the business-use percent. The business basis represents the amount you will be able to depreciate for each item. To find out how much of the business basis can be taken as an expense each year, see the *Family Child Care Tax Workbook*.

New IRS Rule Allows Providers to Deduct Previously Unclaimed Depreciation

Providers can now deduct previously unclaimed depreciation all in one year, according to the new IRS Revenue Ruling 97-37. Previously unclaimed property can include the home, home improvements, appliances, furniture, and large play equipment.

To deduct previously unclaimed depreciation you file **Form 3115 Application for Change in Accounting Method.** There are five major guidelines you must meet the year you file **Form 3115:**

1) You must be in business;

2) You must own the property you want to deduct;

3) You must be using the property you want to deduct in your business;

4) You must file one copy of **Form 3115** by the deadline of the filing of your tax return of the year you want to claim depreciation deductions; and

5) You must file another copy of **Form 3115** with your tax return.

The Impact of Deducting Previously Unclaimed Depreciation under Revenue Procedure 97-37

A provider began her business in 1991, but she did not claim depreciation on her furniture or appliances that she owned at that time. The fair market value of the property she owned in 1991 is listed below. Her Time-Space percentage from 1991 to 1998 was 40 percent. How much would she benefit by claiming this depreciation on **Form 3115?**

Value of property owned in 1991:

Washer	$150	Table/chairs	$500
Dryer	150	Stuffed chair	50
Freezer	50	Bed	200
Refrigerator	200	Stove	200
Sofa	400	Microwave	100

Total value: $2,000 x 40% (Time-Space percentage) = $800 business basis

Using 7-year 200% declining balance depreciation rules:

1991	1992	1993	1994	1995	1996	1997
$800 x 14.29% = $114.32	$800 x 24.49% = $195.92	$800 x 17.49% = $139.92	$800 x 12.49% = $99.92	$800 x 8.93% = $71.44	$800 x 8.92% = $71.36	$800 x 8.93% = $71.44

Total (1991–1997): $764.32

This provider can deduct $764.32 as previously unclaimed depreciation on her 1998 tax return. She must first file **Form 3115** by the due date of her 1998 tax return. She can also claim a depreciation deduction on her 1998 tax return of $35.68.

Teaching Family Child Care Record Keeping and Tax Preparation

Unit F: Miscellaneous Topics

Introduction

One or more of the topics in this section may be included as part of any record-keeping and tax preparation workshop. You can teach these topics separately or in combination with subjects from earlier sections of this curriculum. These topics may be presented at the end of workshops as time allows. Further information about estimated tax, self-employment tax, and retirement planning can be found in *The Basic Guide to Family Child Care Record Keeping* and the *Family Child Care Tax Workbook*. See *The Basic Guide* for further information about pre-tax plans, working with tax preparers, and handling an IRS audit.

Estimated Tax

Providers may have to make quarterly estimated tax payments in order to make sure they pay in 90 percent of their taxes for their family throughout the year. Many providers are not aware of paying quarterly taxes when they begin doing child care. Point out that most providers avoid making quarterly payments by having their spouse increase the spouse's withholding. (See Handouts 1 and 2.)

It is usually difficult for first-year providers to estimate the taxes they will owe by the end of the year. Here is a method to help with this:

1) Estimate the total business income for the year (parent fees plus Food Program reimbursements).

2) Divide the income by two. (Use one-half of the income as a very conservative estimate of business expenses.)

3) Add this new total to last year's tax return to see how much additional taxes are due and whether it is necessary to file estimated tax payments.

Providers often ask what percent of their income they should set aside for estimated tax payments. Since the maximum any provider will have to pay is 43 percent of their net income (15% self-employment tax + 28% federal income tax rate) and most providers can claim many deductions, suggest that providers set aside about 25 percent and they will be safe.

Many providers don't realize that they don't have to make estimated tax payments because the taxes withheld by their spouse this year are greater than the total taxes they paid last year. Put the following illustration on the board:

1997 taxes paid	1998 taxes withheld
$5,000	$5,100

As long as the withholding in 1998 will exceed $5,000, no estimated tax payments are due in 1998. Providers should make sure that their spouse meets the $5,100 goal for 1998.

If the year is well along and not enough estimated tax payments have been made, advise providers to have additional amounts taken out of the spouse's wages. Amounts taken out of any W-2 wages earned as employees will be treated as if it had been withheld throughout the year. Thus there will be no penalties for late estimated tax payments.

Self-Employment Tax

Many providers pay more in self-employment taxes than they do for their business income tax, and this comes as somewhat of a shock. Warn providers that this tax will be due at the time they file their tax return. Self-employment tax is paid on the net profit of the business, not on the gross income. (See Handout 3.)

Make sure you point out that one-half of the amount of the self-employment tax should be entered on **Form 1040**. This will reduce their taxable income. If copies of **Form 1040** are available to providers in the audience, show them the lines where they enter their self-employment tax and one-half of this amount. This reduces the effective self-employment tax rate to 13.07 percent if the provider is in the 15 percent federal tax bracket and to 12.15 percent if the provider is in the 28 percent tax bracket. Tell the audience that for every $1,000 in net profit for their business, they will pay either $121.50 or $130.70 in self-employment taxes.

Pre-Tax Plans

An increasing number of employers are offering flexible benefit plans for their employees. These plans allow parents to set aside some of their salary before taxes to pay for child care expenses. The money set aside is not subject to federal or state taxes and thus parents who participate will lower their taxable income. Employers also benefit by paying less in Social Security taxes on the lower taxable income of their employees.

Parents can save money by participating in a pre-tax plan (see Handout 4). Providers can also benefit from such plans by asking parents to give them any unspent money from their account. Parents who don't spend all the money set aside by the end of the year will forfeit it. Encourage providers to go after this money as a bonus. For example, show that if the parent only spends $2,800 of the $3,000 she sets aside, the extra $200 could be set aside as a bonus for the provider. Providers could tell parents they will spend this money on toys, play equipment, or field trips. (See Handout 5.)

Teaching this topic usually creates a positive impression on providers. Because of this, you may want to insert it during a workshop after a discussion of a difficult topic, such as depreciation or hiring helpers, when the audience might need their spirits lifted.

Retirement Planning

Even though many providers have little money available to set aside for retirement, encourage them to consider contributing to an Individual Retirement Arrangements (IRA). Providers most likely to set up an IRA are group homes, those just starting to make family child caring a career, those who do not have to live off all of their child care income, and those who have been in business for years and are looking for new ways to reduce their taxable income. (See Handouts 6 and 7.)

The main point to cover in talking about retirement plans is that, unlike a regular IRA for which many families are not eligible, providers are always eligible to set up a SEP (Simplified Employee Pension), the new SIMPLE (Savings Incentive Match Plan for Employees of Small Employers), or a Keogh Plan. Many providers are also eligible to set up the new Roth IRA. Because providers can set aside much more money under a SIMPLE than a SEP, it is likely that few providers will establish SEPs in the future. Most banks, credit unions, mutual funds, and brokers can easily set up a SEP, SIMPLE, or Roth IRA for a provider. Many providers do not think much about retirement until they are older, or they count on their spouse's pension. You should strongly recommend that providers take retirement planning seriously, even if it means putting away a very small amount each year. You may want to ask the audience if anyone has already set up a SEP, SIMPLE, or Roth IRA. Providers may see these plans as a more realistic possibility if they know someone who has done it.

Working with Tax Preparers

More and more providers are using tax preparers for their business. Providers should understand that not all tax preparers will act as their advocate and look for every possible deduction. Some preparers will simply take the provider's records and plug in the numbers on the tax forms. Others may be more assertive in making sure the provider has identified every deduction. They may ask, for example, if the provider has recorded all of the hours she worked when the children were not present. Some preparers will offer tax planning assistance to help the provider make financial decisions. Tell providers that they need to select their tax preparer carefully (see Handout 8).

Many providers assume that their tax preparer knows everything about family child care tax issues. Many, in fact, have little experience with family child care tax issues. Stress the fact that tax preparers with a lot of experience in doing personal tax returns are not necessarily informed about filling out **Schedule C** and **Form 8829**. Also, they may be unaware of any changes in the law that may affect the family child care business. Many providers keep their tax preparers up-to-date by giving them the latest edition of the *Family Child Care Tax Workbook* (see also Handout 9).

Be careful in responding to providers who share advice from their tax preparers that appears to be incorrect. If you clearly understand the advice to be bad, explain what is the correct advice and why. Often the tax preparer may not have all the information about a particular provider's circumstances, so recommend that the provider discuss the issue again with the tax preparer. You can also recommend that the provider call the local IRS office and ask for an answer.

Often providers who use tax preparers have little idea of what was done to fill out their tax forms. Emphasize that providers are always responsible for their own tax returns. Providers should take the time to understand what was done to arrive at the numbers on their own tax form. A provider's tax preparer may not be around when the IRS conducts an audit.

Handling an IRS Audit

Most providers are naturally worried about the prospect of an IRS audit. Many are willing to take extremely conservative positions on their tax return to reduce any possibility of an audit. Reassure providers that only a very few are audited and that by keeping careful records, providers should have little to fear. Point out how the IRS chooses providers to audit and the most likely subjects for an audit (see Handout 10).

Occasionally in a workshop, a provider who has been audited will speak about her experiences. If her experiences were positive, point out what the provider did correctly to help ease the others' fears about audits. If the audit experience was a negative one, try to explain why it might have happened and what might have been done differently by the provider (for example, records were kept poorly or the auditor made a mistake). Don't let any negative experiences create a feeling of general pessimism in the workshop. Not all IRS auditors are the same.

Providers are often easily intimidated by audits. Try to encourage providers to be as assertive as possible with auditors because not all are familiar with the family child care business.

Providers must keep records for three years after filing their tax return. Advise providers to keep their records for four years, just to be safe. The IRS usually audits a tax return two to three years after it was filed. After three years have passed, providers need not worry about being audited for that year.

The IRS can audit going back six years if they suspect the provider of fraud or if the provider has underreported her income by more than 25 percent. Warn providers who have operated illegally in the past that they should keep their records for six years, just in case.

Note: Recent IRS policies indicate that they are relying more and more on computers to cross-check tax returns and forms for compliance with tax laws. Because of this, stress the importance of reporting all income and keeping complete and accurate expense records.

Partnerships and Incorporation

More and more providers are forming partnerships or incorporating their business. Many do so before thinking through the consequences of their decision. This is a complex subject area that cannot be adequately covered in a typical record-keeping workshop. See both *The Basic Guide to Family Child Care Record Keeping* and the *Family Child Care Tax Workbook* for further details.

Explain the basic choices for providers who are considering working with another person (see Handout 11). Providers should not form a partnership or incorporate without carefully examining the many pros and cons for each option (see Handout 12). For most providers, the simplest answer is to hire the other person as an employee.

Price Fixing

It is common for providers to talk with each other about their rates, unaware that they are in violation of antitrust laws. Point out this law, stressing that the main problem will arise when providers discuss rates at association meetings. This is because of the greater chance that someone in a larger group will complain about a rate discussion. Providers can ask other providers about their rates as long as the person asking does not identify themselves as a provider. (See Handout 13.)

Estimated Tax

- The IRS requires providers to pay in at least 90 percent of the total taxes their family owes throughout the year.

  $4,000 estimated total taxes owed for 1998
  x 90%
  $3,600 amount that must be paid in throughout 1998

- Estimated taxes are based on the estimated income and expenses for the year. Taxes owed include self-employment tax. If the provider is married and filing jointly, look at the total taxes owed by the family.

- To file estimated taxes, you must pay in one-fourth of your estimated taxes each quarter on April 15, June 15, September 15, and January 15. File **Form 1040 ES**.

- Paying estimated taxes can be avoided if:

  1) You estimate you will receive a tax refund.

  2) You estimate you will owe less than a total of $1,000 in taxes.

  3) You will owe less than 10 percent of your total family taxes by April 15.

  4) The taxes that will be withheld by your spouse in 1998 are greater than the total taxes your family paid in 1997 (unless total adjusted gross income is more than $150,000).

Estimating Your Estimated Tax

STEP 1.
Estimate yearly income.

$300/week x 50 weeks:	$15,000
CACFP reimbursement:	+$3,000
	$18,000

STEP 2.
Estimate yearly expenses. Include all direct expenses, house expenses, and capital expenditures. Subtract from yearly income to find out net income.

yearly expenses:	- $9,000
	$9,000

STEP 3.
Estimate Social Security taxes.

$9,000 net income x 92.35% x 15.3% = $1,271.66

STEP 4.
Estimate federal income tax.

$9,000.00 net income
- $635.83 Social Security tax deduction
$8,364.17 x 15% tax bracket = $1,254.63

STEP 5.
Add up estimated taxes from steps 3 and 4.

$1,271.66	estimated Social Security tax
+$1,254.63	estimated income tax
$2,526.26	estimated total taxes
x 25%	
$631.57	estimated tax payment due each quarter

Self-Employment Tax

- Self-employment tax is owed if the net profit is $400 or more.

  For example:

$1,000	net profit
x 0.9235	amount the net profit is reduced by before self-employment tax is determined
$923.50	amount of net profit taxed
x 15.3%	self-employment tax rate
$141.30	self-employment tax owed

- File self-employment tax on **Schedule SE**.

Note:
Reduce personal taxable income by one-half of self-employment tax amount.

$141.30 ÷ 2 = $70.65

- Put $70.65 on **Form 1040.**

Pre-Tax Plans

Example:
Jane is a parent who is married and has one child. She paid $3,000 in child care expenses in 1997, earned $30,000, and filed a joint tax return.

	No Pre-Tax Plan	Pre-Tax Plan
Calculation of Taxable Income		
Adjusted Gross Income	$30,000	$30,000
Salary Set Aside for Child Care Expenses	-$0	-$3,000
GROSS WAGES	$30,000	$27,000
TAXABLE INCOME	$15,150	$12,150
(after subtracting the standard deductions and personal exemptions)		
Calculation of Federal Taxes		
Gross Wages	$30,000	$27,000
TOTAL TAXES	$3,428	$2,748
(federal income tax and Social Security)		
Child Care Expenses	$3,000 (after tax)	$3,000 (before tax)
NET INCOME	$23,572	$24,252
(after taxes and child care expenses)		

By setting aside $3,000 before taxes, Jane saved $680 in federal taxes. Her employer saved $230 in lower Social Security and Medicare employment taxes.

Child Dependent Care Assistance Programs

Under Internal Revenue Code Sections 125 and 129, employers may establish a dependent care assistance program that allows employee parents to set aside up to $5,000 of their salary for child care costs. Parents do not pay federal or state income taxes on this money they set aside.

Money set aside under such a program must only be used for child care services while the parent is working. Employer programs are usually operated on a calendar year basis, but they may begin and end throughout the year. Parents must elect how much of their salary to set aside before the beginning of the program year. If parents don't spend all of the money they set aside each year, it will be turned over to the parent's employer. Parents may submit child care receipts to their employer up to 90 days after the end of the program year. If the program year ends December 31, 1998, this means the deadline to submit receipts is March 31, 1999.

If parents anticipate having money left over in their dependent care account, they may wish to give it to their child care provider before the year ends. To do so, parents should simply increase the amount they pay their provider. Or the parents could give the unspent money to their child care provider within 90 days after the end of the program year. This can be done by the parent paying the provider the unspent money and then giving the provider another receipt to sign. The receipt should be filled out exactly the same as other receipts (do not identify the payments as a "contribution") and should indicate that the payments are for child care services delivered in the previous year. For example, a receipt filled out in February 1999 might say "$250 for child care services December 15–19, 1998." This receipt represents an extra payment (or bonus) for the excellent services delivered by the provider during the program year.

It is illegal to carry over unspent money to the next program year. It is also illegal to give the provider unspent money and require the provider to return any portion of it to the parent.

Parents should view the giving of any extra money to the provider as an opportunity for the provider to spend it on supplies, training, equipment, or other items that will improve the quality of the child care services made available to their own child.

In order to keep their tax records organized, parents and providers should both sign a receipt at the end of each year that details the amount spent by the parent on child care services. Each person should keep a copy of the receipt. All money received by the provider is taxable income to the provider.

Retirement Plans for Family Child Care Providers

Roth IRA

- Can set aside up to $2,000 (nondeductible) per year

- Can withdraw contributions tax free after 5 years

- Can withdraw interest tax free after age 59 1/2

- Minimum distribution rules at age 70 1/2 do not apply

- Cannot contribute more than $2,000 per person, per year to a Roth IRA, regular IRA, or nondeductible IRA combined

- To contribute to a Roth you must earn less than $110,000 (unmarried) or $160,000 (married, filing jointly)

Savings Incentive Match Plan for Employees of Small Employers (SIMPLE)

- Can set aside up to a little more than $6,000 (deductible) per year of net income

- Operates like a regular IRA

- Must offer same plan to employees earning $5,000 in any of two preceding years

- 25 percent penalty for early withdrawal in first two years

- Cannot make contributions to a SIMPLE and SEP in same year

- Must set up 90 days before end of year

- No income level, everyone is eligible

Simplified Employee Pension (SEP)

- Can set aside up to 12.12 percent of net income per year

- Operates like a regular IRA

- Must offer same plan to employees if employees are over 21 years old, have worked for you in 3 of the past 5 years, and have earned at least $400 in 1997

- Can set up by April 15

- No income level, everyone is eligible

How a Retirement Fund Saves in Taxes

	No Retirement Fund	Roth	SIMPLE	SEP
Net Income	$10,000	$10,000	$10,000	$10,000
Retirement Contribution	0	2,000	6,278	1,212
Taxable Income	10,000	10,000	3,722	8,788
Social Security Tax	1,413	1,413	526	1,242
Income Tax (15%)	1,500	1,500	558	1,318
Total Taxes (15%)	2,913	2,913	1,084	2,560
Income Tax (28%)	2,800	2,800	1,042	2,461
Total Taxes (28%)	4,213	4,213	1,568	3,703
Tax Savings (15%)	—	0	1,829	353
Tax Savings (28%)	—	0	2,645	510

Note:

Interest earned on retirement contributions in a SIMPLE or SEP are subject to taxes upon withdrawal.

© Redleaf National Institute, *Teaching Family Child Care Record Keeping and Tax Preparation: A Curriculum for Trainers* (St. Paul: Redleaf Press, 1998), 1-800-423-8309.

Hiring a Tax Preparer

When hiring a tax preparer, look for the following:

- Professional credentials (Enrolled Agent, CPA, attorney)
- Experience with small business tax returns rather than personal taxes
- Ongoing training in small business tax issues
- Experience doing family child care tax returns
- Willingness to listen to you and explain how your tax return was prepared

Ask the following questions:

- Should I depreciate my home?
- Can I claim hours when children are not present when calculating my Time-Space percentage?
- How do I depreciate my computer and freezer? Are the rules different?

The 8 Key Federal Tax Issues Unique to Family Child Care Providers That Every Provider and Tax Preparer Should Understand

1) The standard for claiming a room in the home as business use is "regular use," not "exclusive use." Child care children need not be present in a room for it to be used regularly for the business (for example, the storage room or laundry room).

2) The garage (attached to the home or not) should be included in the total square feet of the home when calculating the business use of the home. Most family child care providers use their garage on a regular basis for their business because the garage is used as storage (for the vehicle, bicycles, tools, lawn maintenance items, firewood).

3) Providers can claim a higher business-use percent of their home if they have one or more rooms used "exclusively" in their business. Providers should add the space percentage of this exclusive-use area to the Time-Space percentage of the rest of the home to calculate the total business-use percent of the home.

4) When counting the number of hours the home is used for business, include the number of hours child care children are present as well as the number of hours spent on business activities when the child care children are not present. These hours include time spent cleaning, preparing activities, interviewing parents, record keeping, and preparing meals.

5) Reimbursements from the Child and Adult Care Food Program are taxable income to the provider. Reimbursements for the provider's own child (assuming the provider is income-eligible) are not taxable income. Providers are entitled to deduct all food served to child care children, even if the food expense is greater than the Food Program reimbursement.

6) Providers who are not licensed or registered under their state law are still entitled to claim business use of their home expenses if they have applied for or are exempt from mandatory regulations.

© Redleaf National Institute, *Teaching Family Child Care Record Keeping and Tax Preparation: A Curriculum for Trainers* (St. Paul: Redleaf Press, 1998), 1-800-423-8309.

7) All providers are better off financially if they claim depreciation on their home as a business expense. When selling their home, providers must lower the basis of their home by any depreciation they were entitled to claim, whether or not they actually claimed it. Providers must always pay capital gains tax on any house depreciation they claim (or are entitled to claim) after May 6, 1997.

8) Providers must pay capital gains taxes on the business portion of any profit on the sale of their home if they use their home for business in more than 3 of the last 5 years before the date of the sale.

© Redleaf National Institute, *Teaching Family Child Care Record Keeping and Tax Preparation: A Curriculum for Trainers* (St. Paul: Redleaf Press, 1998), 1-800-423-8309.

Common Subjects of IRS Audits

The IRS audits approximately 2 percent of **Schedule C** tax returns each year. How does the IRS choose a provider for an audit?

- Random selection.

- The IRS computer picks out a form because a particular line is not consistent with the rest of the form (for example, $6,000 vehicle expense and $10,000 gross income).

- The IRS will investigate particular industries to discover trends.

Common subjects of audits:

- Food expenses.
  The IRS often denies deductions in excess of CACFP reimbursement.

- Time-Space percentage.
  The IRS often does not allow time spent on business activities when children are not present.

- Shared business and personal expenses.
  The IRS may claim that some business expenses are really personal (particularly household supplies and repairs).

- Vehicle mileage.
  The IRS may deny deductions for business trips to the grocery store.

© Redleaf National Institute, *Teaching Family Child Care Record Keeping and Tax Preparation: A Curriculum for Trainers* (St. Paul: Redleaf Press, 1998), 1-800-423-8309.

When Should Partners Become a "Partnership"?

An increasing number of family child care providers are joining with another provider to offer care out of one home. The two providers may be mother and daughter, friends, or neighbors. They see themselves as equals in their business relationship because they are working together. They share expenses and split the income. They might call themselves partners because neither of them is the boss over the other. There is a problem, however, because the IRS does not approve of these informal types of arrangements. Providers who work together must choose among these four options in running their business:

1) Providers can operate two separate businesses out of one home. Each provider would have separate parent clients and separate contracts with parents. The two businesses would keep completely separate records, although the provider who does not live in the home could pay the other provider some rent for the use of the building. Local licensing rules, however, may prohibit such arrangements.

2) The two providers can set up an employer/employee relationship. Usually the provider who owns the home would be the employer of the business. This method requires the filing of a number of federal and state tax forms for withholding of Social Security, unemployment, and income taxes. The provider/employer would claim all payroll taxes and other expenses as business deductions on her own **Schedule C**.

3) The two providers could form a partnership. This means drafting a partnership agreement that spells out how decisions will be made and how the profit will be divided (it doesn't have to be divided equally). There should be a separate business checking account for the partnership. At the end of the year the partnership needs to file **Form 1065 US Partnership Return of Income** and **Schedule K Partner's Share of Income, Credits, Deductions, etc.** These forms do not create any more tax liability for the two providers. They merely show how the partnership profit is divided, and it is up to each provider to report her own profit and pay her own taxes. The Food Program will issue checks either under the name of the partnership or the individual partners.

© Redleaf National Institute, *Teaching Family Child Care Record Keeping and Tax Preparation: A Curriculum for Trainers* (St. Paul: Redleaf Press, 1998), 1-800-423-8309.

4) The two providers could form a corporation (either a C corporation or an S corporation). To do this requires the filing of formal organizational documents and a series of federal and state tax forms each year. Completely separate records of corporate and personal funds must be kept. The providers would be employees of the corporation and the corporation must file payroll tax forms.

Providers who do not choose one of the above methods and continue to operate as an informal partnership without filing any partnership tax forms run the risk of being audited by the IRS. The IRS may determine that there is an employer/employee relationship and assign penalties and interest for the failure to file payroll tax forms. The employer/employee relationship will be the easiest method to use for most providers who work together. It requires the least paperwork.

For further information before forming a partnership, contact your Food Program, licensing worker (if you have one), and an attorney.

Should a Provider Incorporate?

Advantages

- As a corporation, you can hire yourself as an employee and deduct all wages and payroll taxes as a business expense. The corporation would file all the proper federal and state payroll withholding forms. The provider would report his or her income as an employee on **Form 1040** and not fill out any business forms such as **Schedule C** or **Form 8829.** Doing this will reduce Social Security and Medicare taxes owed because a self-employed person could not deduct his or her Social Security and Medicare taxes as an expense.

- A corporation can provide medical benefits to you as an employee and deduct these costs as a business expense. Your family could also be covered under a family medical benefit.

- Profits from a corporation are only subject to income taxes, while profits from a self-employed business are subject to additional Social Security and Medicare taxes.

- Corporate tax returns may be audited less often than self-employed tax returns.

Disadvantages

- You must pay a professional to set up your corporation and file the proper forms with the state and federal government.

- You must file separate, additional corporate tax forms each year. If you use a tax preparer, the fees to file such forms can be about twice as much as the fees to file your forms as a self-employed person.

- You must keep completely separate business and personal records, with separate checkbooks. Your business records must be organized using balance sheets, and you must follow strict corporate accounting practices. This will probably take more of your time than if you were self-employed.

- The corporation must file all necessary federal and state payroll tax forms. If you use a tax preparer, there will be extra fees for this service.

- There may be additional state taxes owed as an employee of a corporation as compared to a self-employed person.

- A provider who is income-eligible for the Tier I rate on the Food Program cannot be income-eligible as a corporation.

The decision to incorporate is a complex one. You should not incorporate unless you have one or more of the following characteristics:

1) Your family has high medical expenses not covered by existing insurance plans;

2) You are a person who is very good at keeping records; or

3) You plan to be in the child care business for more than just a few years.

When Is it Safe to Talk About Family Child Care Rates?

What do the following situations have in common?

- At an association meeting, family child care providers discuss how much they charge parents.
- In order to find out the going rate in her neighborhood, a new provider calls another provider and asks what she charges parents.
- A family child care association surveys its members about rates and shares the results at the next association meeting.

In all of the above situations, there is a probable violation of the federal antitrust law. What's going on?

Federal antitrust law is designed to encourage competition and discourage competitors from setting prices higher than they would be otherwise. When providers discuss rates at association meetings, this can easily be construed to be a discussion to raise rates. This is true even if there are no direct statements made encouraging providers to raise rates. Associations who operate their own referral service for parents can give parents who call the service rate information, but they cannot share this information with other providers in the association.

Under what circumstances can rate information be shared? Each of these three tests must be met:

1) The individual or organization *other than an association* must collect the rate information and make it readily available to the public, not just to one association.

2) The information must be communicated in such a way as to not allow anyone to identify the rates of any one provider.

3) The sample of providers surveyed must be large enough so that no one can identify the rates of any one provider.

Associations can share rate information collected by resource and referral agencies or by county agencies who use it to determine the subsidy rate for low-income parents. If an association wanted to know what the rates are for a small geographic area, they should have an independent organization do the survey and make sure that the results are widely distributed to the public.

Most associations have unknowingly violated the federal antitrust law. Recently, the Minnesota Attorney General's office investigated one provider association and ordered members to stop sharing rate information at their meetings. After the association promised not to do this in the future, the state took no further action against the association. It is unlikely that a state will ever fine an association that is unknowingly breaking the law.

## Chapter 3

How to Promote and Evaluate Your Training Classes

What to Cover in Your Workshops

Since no trainer can teach everything covered in this curriculum in one workshop, you must decide what to include and what to leave out. There are no absolutes about what should be covered in any workshop. If the audience consists primarily of new providers, you should emphasize topics in the record-keeping, Time-Space percentage, and the business expenses units. If the audience is more experienced, you may want to spend more time on the depreciation and miscellaneous topics units. Workshop audiences usually are made up of providers with a wide range of experience, which makes it difficult to focus your remarks on one particular group.

If you can, find out beforehand what the audience is interested in. The workshop organizer may know of particular issues that they want you to cover. As mentioned in chapter 1, ask your audience what questions they would like answered in the workshop. Allow plenty of time in any workshop for audience questions. At least 25 percent of the time in any workshop should be devoted to answering questions and facilitating audience discussion.

What you cover in your workshops may change according to the time of year. In the spring and summer, the emphasis should be on general record-keeping principles, because providers aren't thinking about filling out their tax forms. In the fall and winter, the emphasis should be on any new IRS rules and tax preparation. Discussing pre-tax plans and retirement plans should be covered in the fall, before the end of the year.

Following are sample agendas for one-hour, two-hour, and three-hour workshops on record keeping and tax preparation. The subject areas and times in these agendas are offered only as suggestions.

Sample Workshop Agendas

One Hour

Time-Space percentage	20 minutes
General record-keeping topics	8 minutes
Deducting food expenses	20 minutes
Overview of key business deductions (vehicle, household supplies)	10 minutes
Pop quiz: deductible expenses for attending the workshop	2 minutes

Two Hours

New IRS rules	5 minutes
Time-Space percentage	20 minutes
General record-keeping topics	10 minutes
Deducting food expenses	20 minutes
Key business deductions (vehicle, household supplies, house expenses)	33 minutes
House depreciation	10 minutes
Helpers	10 minutes
Estimated tax	5 minutes
Working with tax preparers and the IRS	5 minutes
Pop quiz: deductible expenses for attending the workshop	2 minutes

Three Hours

New IRS rules	5 minutes
Time-Space percentage	30 minutes
General record-keeping tips	15 minutes
Deducting food expenses	20 minutes
Key business deductions (vehicle, household supplies, house expenses, gifts, repairs)	43 minutes
House depreciation and selling home	15 minutes
Personal property depreciation	20 minutes
Land and home improvements	5 minutes
Helpers	10 minutes
Estimated tax	5 minutes
Social Security tax	5 minutes
Working with tax preparers and the IRS	5 minutes
Pop quiz: deductible expenses for attending the workshop	2 minutes

How to Promote Your Training

Family child care record keeping and taxes is one of the most requested training topics by family child care providers in every part of the country. Many different organizations offer such training, including family child care associations, Child and Adult Care Food Program sponsors, child care resource and referral agencies, small business development councils, cooperative extension services, community colleges, vocational technical colleges, and child development centers in the military. Contact these organizations in your area, and ask about other groups that might sponsor training.

Many trainers wonder how much to charge for their training. Some trainers charge no fees because training is part of their job with a child care agency. Some tax preparers do training for free in order to attract new clients. Providers should pay something to attend training workshops. The amount may be small ($5–$15), but if providers pay something, it is an acknowledgment that the training has value. Some trainers charge up to $20 per provider for a tax class. Providers who get something for free are less likely to show up or take it seriously. You can easily make the argument that providers will save much more than the cost of the workshop in lower taxes as a result of what is learned. If an organization is paying for the training, the trainer should be paid a fee plus any travel expenses. How much the fee should be depends on local custom and perceived value of the training. Ask the organization if it has a budget for trainers. Tax training usually can command a higher fee than other subjects. Training fees range from $25–$125 per hour of training.

You may want to develop a flyer to help advertise your workshop. On the flyer, identify your strengths as a speaker (for example, "ten years of tax preparation experience, former provider"). Make the flyers available to your sponsoring organization or distribute them yourself if you are putting on the workshop.

Record-Keeping and Tax Preparation Workshop for Family Child Care Providers

Presented by Tom Copeland, author of *The Basic Guide to Family Child Care Record Keeping* and the *Family Child Care Tax Workbook* (published annually). Tom is the leading national authority on family child care tax issues. For ten years his workshops have helped thousands of providers throughout the United States. Tom has a unique ability to present complex issues in easy-to-understand terms.

Record-Keeping and Tax Preparation Workshop covers:
- The latest IRS rulings affecting providers
- The five most important record-keeping rules that can save you money
- Business deductions commonly missed
- How to track food expenses for maximum deduction
- What three rules you should follow when hiring your own children
- How to choose a tax preparer
- How to be assertive with the IRS

DATE: _____

PLACE: _____

COST: _____

FOR FURTHER INFORMATION CALL: _____

SPONSORED BY: _____

How to Use Evaluations to Improve Your Teaching

Every trainer should use workshop evaluations to improve their teaching. You may want to design your own or the organization that sponsors your training may have their own evaluation form. Make sure you ask to see the results of any evaluations collected for your workshop.

No one likes criticism. It is also impossible to please everyone. Use evaluations to help identify your weaknesses and improve your presentation. If several people comment that you didn't allow time for enough questions, pay more attention to this. Look for comments that suggest how you might do a better job. If the negative comments seem to be isolated or unfair, don't dwell on them. If someone writes a particularly positive comment, save it and use it on a flyer to advertise the training you offer.

The following are two sample evaluation forms. The first evaluation form asks participants to respond to a few questions and gives them the opportunity to write down their comments. The second evaluation form is more unusual. You can use it to test how much the participants learned from the workshop. Ask everyone to answer the ten questions before you begin the workshop. Have them put their answer in the left column. At the end of the workshop, ask them to answer the same questions again and put their answers in the right column. Collect the results at the end of the workshop. Measure any differences in the answers and use the results to promote your abilities as a trainer. You will want to change some of the questions as the subjects of your workshops change.

Record-Keeping and Tax Preparation
Workshop Evaluation

Please take a moment to fill out this evaluation so we can improve our future workshops.

1) Overall, I would rate this workshop (check one):

   Excellent_____ Very Good_____ Good _____ Fair_____ Poor_____

2) Rate the trainer in the following areas:

	excellent	very good	good	fair	poor
Knowledge of the subject	_____	_____	_____	_____	_____
Ability to present and explain material	_____	_____	_____	_____	_____
Ability to sustain interest throughout the session	_____	_____	_____	_____	_____
Responsiveness to questions and concerns	_____	_____	_____	_____	_____

3) What was the most useful aspect of the workshop?

4) How could this workshop be improved?

5) Other comments:

© Redleaf National Institute, *Teaching Family Child Care Record Keeping and Tax Preparation: A Curriculum for Trainers* (St. Paul: Redleaf Press, 1998), 1-800-423-8309.

Record-Keeping and Tax Preparation
Workshop Evaluation

Instructions: Before the workshop begins, please take a moment to answer the questions below in the first column. At the end of the workshop you will be asked to answer them again in the second column. Your answers will help us improve future workshops.

	Answer before workshop begins			Answer after workshop is over		
	true (T)	false (F)	don't know (DK)	true (T)	false (F)	don't know (DK)
1) Providers must keep a log in their vehicle to record odometer readings for business trips.	(T)	(F)	(DK)	(T)	(F)	(DK)
2) Providers may count the hours spent cleaning their home for their business in their Time-Space calculation.	(T)	(F)	(DK)	(T)	(F)	(DK)
3) Providers may count the hours spent shopping or in training seminars in their Time-Space calculation.	(T)	(F)	(DK)	(T)	(F)	(DK)
4) Providers may claim up to $25 per person for gifts for their child care parents as a business expense.	(T)	(F)	(DK)	(T)	(F)	(DK)
5) Providers should treat substitutes in their business as employees.	(T)	(F)	(DK)	(T)	(F)	(DK)
6) The rules for depreciating a TV, a computer, and a refrigerator are the same.	(T)	(F)	(DK)	(T)	(F)	(DK)
7) Some providers should not depreciate their home.	(T)	(F)	(DK)	(T)	(F)	(DK)
8) All providers must file quarterly estimated tax payments.	(T)	(F)	(DK)	(T)	(F)	(DK)
9) Most providers are eligible to set up a Simplified Employee Pension.	(T)	(F)	(DK)	(T)	(F)	(DK)
10) Food expenses are a common subject of IRS audits.	(T)	(F)	(DK)	(T)	(F)	(DK)

© Redleaf National Institute, *Teaching Family Child Care Record Keeping and Tax Preparation: A Curriculum for Trainers* (St. Paul: Redleaf Press, 1998), 1-800-423-8309.

Appendix

IRS Forms and Publications for the Family Child Care Business

You must prepare your tax forms in the following order:
Form 4562 Depreciation and Amortization
Schedule C Profit or Loss from Business
Form 8829 Expenses for Business Use of Your Home
Schedule SE Self-Employment Tax
Form 1040 U.S. Individual Income Tax Return

Other forms and publications:
Form 1040 ES Estimated Tax for Individuals
Form W-10 Dependent Care Provider's Identification and Certification
Form 1040X Amended U.S. Individual Tax Return (*if necessary*)
Form 3115 Application for change in Accounting Method
Form 5305-SEP Simplified Employee Pension
Form 8826 Disabled Access Credit
Form 4797 Sales of Business Property
Form 4684 Casualties and Thefts
Form 2119 Sale of Your Home
Form 8109 Federal Tax Deposit Coupon
Schedule EIC Earned Income Credit
Schedule A Itemized Deductions
Schedule B Interest and Dividend Income
Schedule D Capital Gains and Losses
Publication 505 Tax Withholding and Estimated Tax
Publication 583 Taxpayers Starting a Business
Publication 587 Business Use of Your Home (*reproduced below*)
Publication 334 Tax Guide for Small Business
Publication 917 Business Use of a Car (*reproduced below*)
Publication 590 Individual Retirement Arrangements
Publication 534 Depreciation (*reproduced below*)
Publication 556 Examination of Returns, Appeal Rights, and Claims for Refund
Publication 544 Sales and Other Dispositions of Assets

For employees:
Form W-2 Wages and Tax Statement
Form W-4 Employee's Withholding Allowance Certificate
Form W-3 Transmittal of Income and Tax Statements
Form 940 Employer's Annual Federal Unemployment Tax Return (FUTA)
Form 941 Employer's Quarterly Federal Tax Return
Form SS-4 Application for Employer Identification Number
Form 1099 Miscellaneous Income
Form I-9 Employment Eligibility Verification
Circular E Employer's Tax Guide

You can find IRS forms and publications at local IRS offices, banks, libraries, and post offices. Or you can call 1-800-829-3676 to have IRS forms mailed to you. You can also get forms faxed to you by calling 703-487-4160. The IRS has a Web site where you can download any form, publication, or instructions. Their address is www.irs.ustreas.gov.

Form **4562**

Department of the Treasury
Internal Revenue Service   (99)

Depreciation and Amortization
(Including Information on Listed Property)

▶ **See separate instructions.**   ▶ **Attach this form to your return.**

OMB No. 1545-0172

1998

Attachment
Sequence No. **67**

Name(s) shown on return	Business or activity to which this form relates	Identifying number

Part I	Election To Expense Certain Tangible Property (Section 179) (Note: *If you have any "listed property," complete Part V before you complete Part I.*)		

1	Maximum dollar limitation. If an enterprise zone business, see page 2 of the instructions . .	**1**	$18,500
2	Total cost of section 179 property placed in service. See page 2 of the instructions	**2**	
3	Threshold cost of section 179 property before reduction in limitation	**3**	$200,000
4	Reduction in limitation. Subtract line 3 from line 2. If zero or less, enter -0-	**4**	
5	Dollar limitation for tax year. Subtract line 4 from line 1. If zero or less, enter -0-. If married filing separately, see page 2 of the instructions	**5**	

(a) Description of property	**(b)** Cost (business use only)	**(c)** Elected cost
6		

7	Listed property. Enter amount from line 27.	**7**	
8	Total elected cost of section 179 property. Add amounts in column (c), lines 6 and 7 . . .	**8**	
9	Tentative deduction. Enter the smaller of line 5 or line 8	**9**	
10	Carryover of disallowed deduction from 1997. See page 3 of the instructions	**10**	
11	Business income limitation. Enter the smaller of business income (not less than zero) or line 5 (see instructions)	**11**	
12	Section 179 expense deduction. Add lines 9 and 10, but do not enter more than line 11 . .	**12**	
13	Carryover of disallowed deduction to 1999. Add lines 9 and 10, less line 12 ▶	**13**	

Note: *Do not use Part II or Part III below for listed property (automobiles, certain other vehicles, cellular telephones, certain computers, or property used for entertainment, recreation, or amusement). Instead, use Part V for listed property.*

Part II	MACRS Depreciation For Assets Placed in Service ONLY During Your 1998 Tax Year (Do Not Include Listed Property.)

Section A—General Asset Account Election

14   If you are making the election under section 168(i)(4) to group any assets placed in service during the tax year into one or more general asset accounts, check this box. See page 3 of the instructions . . . . ▶ ☐

Section B—General Depreciation System (GDS) (See page 3 of the instructions.)

(a) Classification of property	**(b)** Month and year placed in service	**(c)** Basis for depreciation (business/investment use only—see instructions)	**(d)** Recovery period	**(e)** Convention	**(f)** Method	**(g)** Depreciation deduction
15a 3-year property						
b 5-year property						
c 7-year property						
d 10-year property						
e 15-year property						
f 20-year property						
g 25-year property			25 yrs.		S/L	
h Residential rental property			27.5 yrs.	MM	S/L	
			27.5 yrs.	MM	S/L	
i Nonresidential real property			39 yrs.	MM	S/L	
				MM	S/L	

Section C—Alternative Depreciation System (ADS) (See page 5 of the instructions.)

16a Class life					S/L	
b 12-year			12 yrs.		S/L	
c 40-year			40 yrs.	MM	S/L	

Part III	Other Depreciation (Do Not Include Listed Property.) (See page 6 of the instructions.)

17	GDS and ADS deductions for assets placed in service in tax years beginning before 1998	**17**	
18	Property subject to section 168(f)(1) election	**18**	
19	ACRS and other depreciation	**19**	

Part IV	Summary (See page 6 of the instructions.)

20	Listed property. Enter amount from line 26.	**20**	
21	**Total.** Add deductions on line 12, lines 15 and 16 in column (g), and lines 17 through 20. Enter here and on the appropriate lines of your return. Partnerships and S corporations—see instructions . .	**21**	
22	For assets shown above and placed in service during the current year, enter the portion of the basis attributable to section 263A costs	**22**	

Part V   Listed Property—Automobiles, Certain Other Vehicles, Cellular Telephones, Certain Computers, and Property Used for Entertainment, Recreation, or Amusement

Note: *For any vehicle for which you are using the standard mileage rate or deducting lease expense, complete **only** 23a, 23b, columns (a) through (c) of Section A, all of Section B, and Section C if applicable.*

Section A—Depreciation and Other Information (Caution: *See page 8 of the instructions for limits for passenger automobiles.*)

23a Do you have evidence to support the business/investment use claimed? ☐ **Yes** ☐ **No**   23b If "Yes," is the evidence written? ☐ **Yes** ☐ **No**

(a) Type of property (list vehicles first)	(b) Date placed in service	(c) Business/ investment use percentage	(d) Cost or other basis	(e) Basis for depreciation (business/investment use only)	(f) Recovery period	(g) Method/ Convention	(h) Depreciation deduction	(i) Elected section 179 cost
24 Property used more than 50% in a qualified business use (See page 7 of the instructions.):								
		%						
		%						
		%						
25 Property used 50% or less in a qualified business use (See page 7 of the instructions.):								
		%				S/L –		
		%				S/L –		
		%				S/L –		

26 Add amounts in column (h). Enter the total here and on line 20, page 1 . . . . .   **26**

27 Add amounts in column (i). Enter the total here and on line 7, page 1 . . . .   **27**

Section B—Information on Use of Vehicles

Complete this section for vehicles used by a sole proprietor, partner, or other "more than 5% owner," or related person.
If you provided vehicles to your employees, first answer the questions in Section C to see if you meet an exception to completing this section for those vehicles.

		(a) Vehicle 1		(b) Vehicle 2		(c) Vehicle 3		(d) Vehicle 4		(e) Vehicle 5		(f) Vehicle 6	
28	Total business/investment miles driven during the year (DO NOT include commuting miles)												
29	Total commuting miles driven during the year												
30	Total other personal (noncommuting) miles driven												
31	Total miles driven during the year. Add lines 28 through 30.												
		Yes	No	Yes	No	Yes	No	Yes	No	Yes	No	Yes	No
32	Was the vehicle available for personal use during off-duty hours?												
33	Was the vehicle used primarily by a more than 5% owner or related person?												
34	Is another vehicle available for personal use?												

Section C—Questions for Employers Who Provide Vehicles for Use by Their Employees

*Answer these questions to determine if you meet an exception to completing Section B for vehicles used by employees who are **not** more than 5% owners or related persons.*

		Yes	No
35	Do you maintain a written policy statement that prohibits all personal use of vehicles, including commuting, by your employees?		
36	Do you maintain a written policy statement that prohibits personal use of vehicles, except commuting, by your employees? See page 9 of the instructions for vehicles used by corporate officers, directors, or 1% or more owners		
37	Do you treat all use of vehicles by employees as personal use?		
38	Do you provide more than five vehicles to your employees, obtain information from your employees about the use of the vehicles, and retain the information received?		
39	Do you meet the requirements concerning qualified automobile demonstration use? See page 9 of the instructions . .		

Note: *If your answer to 35, 36, 37, 38, or 39 is "Yes," you need not complete Section B for the covered vehicles.*

Part VI   Amortization

(a) Description of costs	(b) Date amortization begins	(c) Amortizable amount	(d) Code section	(e) Amortization period or percentage	(f) Amortization for this year
40 Amortization of costs that begins during your 1998 tax year:					

41 Amortization of costs that began before 1998 . . . .   **41**

42 **Total.** Enter here and on "Other Deductions" or "Other Expenses" line of your return . . .   **42**

SCHEDULE C
(Form 1040)

Department of the Treasury
Internal Revenue Service   (99)

Profit or Loss From Business
(Sole Proprietorship)
▶ **Partnerships, joint ventures, etc., must file Form 1065 or Form 1065-B.**
▶ **Attach to Form 1040 or Form 1041.**   ▶ **See Instructions for Schedule C (Form 1040).**

OMB No. 1545-0074

19**98**

Attachment
Sequence No. **09**

Name of proprietor	Social security number (SSN)

A	Principal business or profession, including product or service (see page C-1)	B Enter NEW code from pages C-8 & 9 ▶

C	Business name. If no separate business name, leave blank.	D Employer ID number (EIN), if any

E   Business address (including suite or room no.) ▶ ....
      City, town or post office, state, and ZIP code

F   Accounting method: **(1)** ☐ Cash   **(2)** ☐ Accrual   **(3)** ☐ Other (specify) ▶ ....

G   Did you "materially participate" in the operation of this business during 1998? If "No," see page C-2 for limit on losses   . ☐ Yes ☐ No

H   If you started or acquired this business during 1998, check here   . . . . ▶ ☐

Part I   Income

1	Gross receipts or sales. **Caution:** *If this income was reported to you on Form W-2 and the "Statutory employee" box on that form was checked, see page C-3 and check here* . . . . . . ▶ ☐	1	
2	Returns and allowances	2	
3	Subtract line 2 from line 1	3	
4	Cost of goods sold (from line 42 on page 2)	4	
5	**Gross profit.** Subtract line 4 from line 3	5	
6	Other income, including Federal and state gasoline or fuel tax credit or refund (see page C-3) . . .	6	
7	**Gross income.** Add lines 5 and 6 . . . . ▶	7	

Part II   Expenses. Enter expenses for business use of your home **only** on line 30.

8	Advertising	8		19 Pension and profit-sharing plans	19	
9	Bad debts from sales or services (see page C-3) . .	9		20 Rent or lease (see page C-5):		
				a Vehicles, machinery, and equipment .	20a	
10	Car and truck expenses (see page C-3)	10		**b** Other business property . .	20b	
11	Commissions and fees . .	11		21 Repairs and maintenance . .	21	
12	Depletion	12		22 Supplies (not included in Part III) .	22	
13	Depreciation and section 179 expense deduction (not included in Part III) (see page C-4) . .	13		23 Taxes and licenses	23	
				24 Travel, meals, and entertainment:		
				a Travel	24a	
14	Employee benefit programs (other than on line 19) . . .	14		**b** Meals and en-tertainment .		
15	Insurance (other than health) .	15		**c** Enter 50% of line 24b subject to limitations (see page C-6) .		
16	Interest:					
a	Mortgage (paid to banks, etc.) .	16a		**d** Subtract line 24c from line 24b	24d	
b	Other	16b		25 Utilities	25	
17	Legal and professional services	17		26 Wages (less employment credits) .	26	
				27 Other expenses (from line 48 on page 2)	27	
18	Office expense	18				

28	**Total expenses** before expenses for business use of home. Add lines 8 through 27 in columns . ▶	28	
29	Tentative profit (loss). Subtract line 28 from line 7	29	
30	Expenses for business use of your home. Attach **Form 8829**	30	
31	**Net profit or (loss).** Subtract line 30 from line 29.		
	• If a profit, enter on **Form 1040, line 12,** and ALSO on **Schedule SE, line 2** (statutory employees, see page C-6). Estates and trusts, enter on Form 1041, line 3.	31	
	• If a loss, you MUST go on to line 32.		
32	If you have a loss, check the box that describes your investment in this activity (see page C-6).		
	• If you checked 32a, enter the loss on **Form 1040, line 12,** and ALSO on **Schedule SE, line 2** (statutory employees, see page C-6). Estates and trusts, enter on Form 1041, line 3.	32a ☐ All investment is at risk.	
		32b ☐ Some investment is not at risk.	
	• If you checked 32b, you MUST attach **Form 6198.**		

Part III **Cost of Goods Sold** (see page C-7)

33 Method(s) used to
value closing inventory: **a** ☐ Cost   **b** ☐ Lower of cost or market   **c** ☐ Other (attach explanation)

34 Was there any change in determining quantities, costs, or valuations between opening and closing inventory? If
"Yes," attach explanation . . . . ☐ **Yes**   ☐ **No**

35 Inventory at beginning of year. If different from last year's closing inventory, attach explanation . .	35	
36 Purchases less cost of items withdrawn for personal use	36	
37 Cost of labor. Do not include any amounts paid to yourself	37	
38 Materials and supplies	38	
39 Other costs	39	
40 Add lines 35 through 39	40	
41 Inventory at end of year	41	
42 **Cost of goods sold.** Subtract line 41 from line 40. Enter the result here and on page 1, line 4 . .	42	

Part IV **Information on Your Vehicle.** Complete this part **ONLY** if you are claiming car or truck expenses on line 10 and are not required to file Form 4562 for this business. See the instructions for line 13 on page C-4 to find out if you must file.

43 When did you place your vehicle in service for business purposes? (month, day, year) ▶ ..../.........../........ .

44 Of the total number of miles you drove your vehicle during 1998, enter the number of miles you used your vehicle for:

a Business .... **b** Commuting .... **c** Other ....

45 Do you (or your spouse) have another vehicle available for personal use?. . . . . ☐ **Yes**   ☐ **No**

46 Was your vehicle available for use during off-duty hours? . . . . ☐ **Yes**   ☐ **No**

47a Do you have evidence to support your deduction? . . . . ☐ **Yes**   ☐ **No**

 b If "Yes," is the evidence written? . . . . ☐ **Yes**   ☐ **No**

Part V **Other Expenses.** List below business expenses not included on lines 8–26 or line 30.

------------------------------		
48 **Total other expenses.** Enter here and on page 1, line 27	48	

Expenses for Business Use of Your Home

▶ File only with Schedule C (Form 1040). Use a separate Form 8829 for each home you used for business during the year.

▶ See separate instructions.

OMB No. 1545-1266

1998

Attachment
Sequence No. **66**

Name(s) of proprietor(s) | Your social security number

Part I Part of Your Home Used for Business

1	Area used regularly and exclusively for business, regularly for day care, or for storage of inventory or product samples. See instructions	1	
2	Total area of home	2	
3	Divide line 1 by line 2. Enter the result as a percentage	3	%

- For day-care facilities not used exclusively for business, also complete lines 4–6.
- All others, skip lines 4–6 and enter the amount from line 3 on line 7.

4	Multiply days used for day care during year by hours used per day .	4	hr.
5	Total hours available for use during the year (365 days × 24 hours). See instructions	5	8,760 hr.
6	Divide line 4 by line 5. Enter the result as a decimal amount	6	.
7	Business percentage. For day-care facilities not used exclusively for business, multiply line 6 by line 3 (enter the result as a percentage). All others, enter the amount from line 3 . . . . ▶	7	%

Part II Figure Your Allowable Deduction

8	Enter the amount from Schedule C, line 29, **plus** any net gain or (loss) derived from the business use of your home and shown on Schedule D or Form 4797. If more than one place of business, see instructions		8	

See instructions for columns (a) and (b) before completing lines 9–20.

		(a) Direct expenses	(b) Indirect expenses		
9	Casualty losses. See instructions	9			
10	Deductible mortgage interest. See instructions	10			
11	Real estate taxes. See instructions	11			
12	Add lines 9, 10, and 11	12			
13	Multiply line 12, column (b) by line 7		13		
14	Add line 12, column (a) and line 13			14	
15	Subtract line 14 from line 8. If zero or less, enter -0-			15	
16	Excess mortgage interest. See instructions	16			
17	Insurance	17			
18	Repairs and maintenance	18			
19	Utilities	19			
20	Other expenses. See instructions	20			
21	Add lines 16 through 20	21			
22	Multiply line 21, column (b) by line 7		22		
23	Carryover of operating expenses from 1997 Form 8829, line 41		23		
24	Add line 21 in column (a), line 22, and line 23			24	
25	Allowable operating expenses. Enter the **smaller** of line 15 or line 24			25	
26	Limit on excess casualty losses and depreciation. Subtract line 25 from line 15			26	
27	Excess casualty losses. See instructions		27		
28	Depreciation of your home from Part III below		28		
29	Carryover of excess casualty losses and depreciation from 1997 Form 8829, line 42		29		
30	Add lines 27 through 29			30	
31	Allowable excess casualty losses and depreciation. Enter the **smaller** of line 26 or line 30			31	
32	Add lines 14, 25, and 31			32	
33	Casualty loss portion, if any, from lines 14 and 31. Carry amount to **Form 4684,** Section B			33	
34	Allowable expenses for business use of your home. Subtract line 33 from line 32. Enter here and on Schedule C, line 30. If your home was used for more than one business, see instructions ▶			34	

Part III Depreciation of Your Home

35	Enter the **smaller** of your home's adjusted basis or its fair market value. See instructions	35	
36	Value of land included on line 35	36	
37	Basis of building. Subtract line 36 from line 35	37	
38	Business basis of building. Multiply line 37 by line 7	38	
39	Depreciation percentage. See instructions	39	%
40	Depreciation allowable. Multiply line 38 by line 39. Enter here and on line 28 above. See instructions	40	

Part IV Carryover of Unallowed Expenses to 1999

41	Operating expenses. Subtract line 25 from line 24. If less than zero, enter -0-	41	
42	Excess casualty losses and depreciation. Subtract line 31 from line 30. If less than zero, enter -0-	42	

SCHEDULE SE	Self-Employment Tax	OMB No. 1545-0074
(Form 1040)	▶ See Instructions for Schedule SE (Form 1040).	**1998**
Department of the Treasury Internal Revenue Service	▶ **Attach to Form 1040.**	Attachment Sequence No. **17**

Name of person with **self-employment** income (as shown on Form 1040)	Social security number of person with **self-employment** income ▶	

Who Must File Schedule SE

You must file Schedule SE if:

- You had net earnings from self-employment from **other than** church employee income (line 4 of Short Schedule SE or line 4c of Long Schedule SE) of $400 or more, **OR**
- You had church employee income of $108.28 or more. Income from services you performed as a minister or a member of a religious order **is not** church employee income. See page SE-1.

Note: *Even if you had a loss or a small amount of income from self-employment, it may be to your benefit to file Schedule SE and use either "optional method" in Part II of Long Schedule SE. See page SE-3.*

Exception. If your only self-employment income was from earnings as a minister, member of a religious order, or Christian Science practitioner **and** you filed Form 4361 and received IRS approval not to be taxed on those earnings, **do not** file Schedule SE. Instead, write "Exempt–Form 4361" on Form 1040, line 50.

May I Use Short Schedule SE or MUST I Use Long Schedule SE?

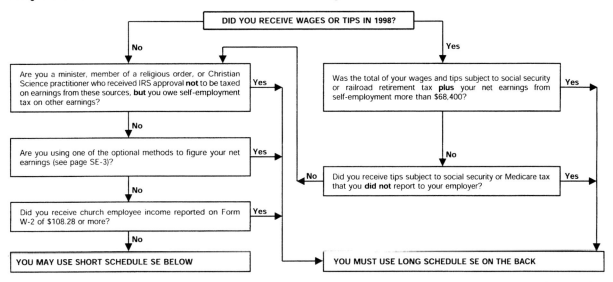

Section A—Short Schedule SE. Caution: *Read above to see if you can use Short Schedule SE.*

1	Net farm profit or (loss) from Schedule F, line 36, and farm partnerships, Schedule K-1 (Form 1065), line 15a	**1**	
2	Net profit or (loss) from Schedule C, line 31; Schedule C-EZ, line 3; Schedule K-1 (Form 1065), line 15a (other than farming); and Schedule K-1 (Form 1065-B), box 9. Ministers and members of religious orders, see page SE-1 for amounts to report on this line. See page SE-2 for other income to report	**2**	
3	Combine lines 1 and 2	**3**	
4	**Net earnings from self-employment.** Multiply line 3 by 92.35% (.9235). If less than $400, **do not** file this schedule; you do not owe self-employment tax . . . . ▶	**4**	
5	**Self-employment tax.** If the amount on line 4 is: • $68,400 or less, multiply line 4 by 15.3% (.153). Enter the result here and on **Form 1040, line 50.** • More than $68,400, multiply line 4 by 2.9% (.029). Then, add $8,481.60 to the result. Enter the total here and on **Form 1040, line 50.**	**5**	
6	**Deduction for one-half of self-employment tax.** Multiply line 5 by 50% (.5). Enter the result here and on **Form 1040, line 27**	**6**		

Form 1040

Department of the Treasury—Internal Revenue Service

U.S. Individual Income Tax Return 1998

(99) IRS Use Only—Do not write or staple in this space.

For the year Jan. 1–Dec. 31, 1998, or other tax year beginning _____, 1998, ending _____, 19___ OMB No. 1545-0074

Label

(See instructions on page 18.)

Use the IRS label. Otherwise, please print or type.

LABEL HERE

Your first name and initial	Last name	Your social security number
If a joint return, spouse's first name and initial	Last name	Spouse's social security number

Home address (number and street). If you have a P.O. box, see page 18. Apt. no.

City, town or post office, state, and ZIP code. If you have a foreign address, see page 18.

▲ **IMPORTANT!** ▲
You **must** enter your SSN(s) above.

Presidential Election Campaign
(See page 18.)

▶ Do you want $3 to go to this fund? . . . .
If a joint return, does your spouse want $3 to go to this fund? . . . .

	Yes	No

Note: Checking "Yes" will not change your tax or reduce your refund.

Filing Status

Check only one box.

1 ☐ Single
2 ☐ Married filing joint return (even if only one had income)
3 ☐ Married filing separate return. Enter spouse's social security no. above and full name here. ▶ _____
4 ☐ Head of household (with qualifying person). (See page 18.) If the qualifying person is a child but not your dependent, enter this child's name here. ▶ _____
5 ☐ Qualifying widow(er) with dependent child (year spouse died ▶ 19___). (See page 18.)

Exemptions

If more than six dependents, see page 19.

6a ☐ **Yourself.** If your parent (or someone else) can claim you as a dependent on his or her tax return, **do not** check box 6a. . . . .

b ☐ **Spouse** . . . .

c **Dependents:**

(1) First name Last name	(2) Dependent's social security number	(3) Dependent's relationship to you	(4) ✔ if qualifying child for child tax credit (see page 19)
_____	_____	_____	☐
_____	_____	_____	☐
_____	_____	_____	☐
_____	_____	_____	☐
_____	_____	_____	☐
_____	_____	_____	☐

No. of boxes checked on 6a and 6b ____

No. of your children on 6c who:
- lived with you ____
- did not live with you due to divorce or separation (see page 19) ____

Dependents on 6c not entered above ____

Add numbers entered on lines above ▶ ☐

d Total number of exemptions claimed . . . .

Income

Attach Copy B of your Forms W-2, W-2G, and 1099-R here.

If you did not get a W-2, see page 20.

Enclose, but do not staple, any payment. Also, please use **Form 1040-V.**

7	Wages, salaries, tips, etc. Attach Form(s) W-2	**7**
8a	**Taxable** interest. Attach Schedule B if required	**8a**
b	**Tax-exempt** interest. DO NOT include on line 8a . . . **8b**	
9	Ordinary dividends. Attach Schedule B if required	**9**
10	Taxable refunds, credits, or offsets of state and local income taxes (see page 21) . .	**10**
11	Alimony received	**11**
12	Business income or (loss). Attach Schedule C or C-EZ	**12**
13	Capital gain or (loss). Attach Schedule D	**13**
14	Other gains or (losses). Attach Form 4797	**14**
15a	Total IRA distributions . **15a**	b Taxable amount (see page 22)	**15b**
16a	Total pensions and annuities **16a**	b Taxable amount (see page 22)	**16b**
17	Rental real estate, royalties, partnerships, S corporations, trusts, etc. Attach Schedule E	**17**
18	Farm income or (loss). Attach Schedule F	**18**
19	Unemployment compensation	**19**
20a	Social security benefits . **20a**	b Taxable amount (see page 24)	**20b**
21	Other income. List type and amount—see page 24 _____	**21**
22	Add the amounts in the far right column for lines 7 through 21. This is your **total income** ▶	**22**

Adjusted Gross Income

If line 33 is under $30,095 (under $10,030 if a child did not live with you), see EIC inst. on page 36.

23	IRA deduction (see page 25)	**23**	
24	Student loan interest deduction (see page 27)	**24**	
25	Medical savings account deduction. Attach Form 8853 .	**25**	
26	Moving expenses. Attach Form 3903	**26**	
27	One-half of self-employment tax. Attach Schedule SE .	**27**	
28	Self-employed health insurance deduction (see page 28)	**28**	
29	Keogh and self-employed SEP and SIMPLE plans . .	**29**	
30	Penalty on early withdrawal of savings	**30**	
31a	Alimony paid b Recipient's SSN ▶ _____	**31a**	
32	Add lines 23 through 31a		**32**
33	Subtract line 32 from line 22. This is your **adjusted gross income** . . . . . ▶		**33**

Teaching Family Child Care Record Keeping and Tax Preparation

Tax and Credits	**34**	Amount from line 33 (adjusted gross income)	**34**	
	35a	Check if: ☐ **You** were 65 or older, ☐ Blind; ☐ **Spouse** was 65 or older, ☐ Blind. Add the number of boxes checked above and enter the total here . . . . ▶ **35a**		
	b	If you are married filing separately and your spouse itemizes deductions or you were a dual-status alien, see page 29 and check here . . . . . ▶ **35b** ☐		
Standard Deduction for Most People	**36**	Enter the **larger** of your **itemized deductions** from Schedule A, line 28, **OR standard deduction** shown on the left. **But** see page 30 to find your standard deduction if you checked any box on line 35a or 35b **or** if someone can claim you as a dependent . .	**36**	
Single: $4,250	**37**	Subtract line 36 from line 34	**37**	
Head of household: $6,250	**38**	If line 34 is $93,400 or less, multiply $2,700 by the total number of exemptions claimed on line 6d. If line 34 is over $93,400, see the worksheet on page 30 for the amount to enter .	**38**	
Married filing jointly or Qualifying widow(er): $7,100	**39**	**Taxable income.** Subtract line 38 from line 37. If line 38 is more than line 37, enter -0- .	**39**	
	40	**Tax.** See page 30. Check if any tax from **a** ☐ Form(s) 8814 **b** ☐ Form 4972 . . ▶	**40**	
Married filing separately: $3,550	**41**	Credit for child and dependent care expenses. Attach Form 2441	**41**	
	42	Credit for the elderly or the disabled. Attach Schedule R . .	**42**	
	43	Child tax credit (see page 31)	**43**	
	44	Education credits. Attach Form 8863	**44**	
	45	Adoption credit. Attach Form 8839	**45**	
	46	Foreign tax credit. Attach Form 1116 if required . . .	**46**	
	47	Other. Check if from **a** ☐ Form 3800 **b** ☐ Form 8396 **c** ☐ Form 8801 **d** ☐ Form (specify) _____	**47**	
	48	Add lines 41 through 47. These are your **total credits** . . .	**48**	
	49	Subtract line 48 from line 40. If line 48 is more than line 40, enter -0- . . . . . ▶	**49**	
Other Taxes	**50**	Self-employment tax. Attach Schedule SE	**50**	
	51	Alternative minimum tax. Attach Form 6251	**51**	
	52	Social security and Medicare tax on tip income not reported to employer. Attach Form 4137	**52**	
	53	Tax on IRAs, other retirement plans, and MSAs. Attach Form 5329 if required	**53**	
	54	Advance earned income credit payments from Form(s) W-2	**54**	
	55	Household employment taxes. Attach Schedule H	**55**	
	56	Add lines 49 through 55. This is your **total tax** . . . . ▶	**56**	
Payments	**57**	Federal income tax withheld from Forms W-2 and 1099 . .	**57**	
	58	1998 estimated tax payments and amount applied from 1997 return .	**58**	
Attach Forms W-2 and W-2G on the front. Also attach Form 1099-R if tax was withheld.	**59a**	**Earned income credit.** Attach Schedule EIC if you have a qualifying child **b** Nontaxable earned income: amount ▶ [ ] and type ▶ _____	**59a**	
	60	Additional child tax credit. Attach Form 8812	**60**	
	61	Amount paid with Form 4868 (request for extension) . .	**61**	
	62	Excess social security and RRTA tax withheld (see page 43)	**62**	
	63	Other payments. Check if from **a** ☐ Form 2439 **b** ☐ Form 4136	**63**	
	64	Add lines 57, 58, 59a, and 60 through 63. These are your **total payments** . . . . ▶	**64**	
Refund	**65**	If line 64 is more than line 56, subtract line 56 from line 64. This is the amount you **OVERPAID**	**65**	
	66a	Amount of line 65 you want **REFUNDED TO YOU.** . . . . ▶	**66a**	
Have it directly deposited! See page 44 and fill in 66b, 66c, and 66d.	▶ **b**	Routing number [ ] ▶ **c** Type: ☐ Checking ☐ Savings		
	▶ **d**	Account number [ ]		
	67	Amount of line 65 you want **APPLIED TO YOUR 1999 ESTIMATED TAX** ▶ [67]		
Amount You Owe	**68**	If line 56 is more than line 64, subtract line 64 from line 56. This is the **AMOUNT YOU OWE.** For details on how to pay, see page 44 . . . . ▶	**68**	
	69	Estimated tax penalty. Also include on line 68 . . . . [69]		

Sign Here

Joint return? See page 18. Keep a copy for your records.

Under penalties of perjury, I declare that I have examined this return and accompanying schedules and statements, and to the best of my knowledge and belief, they are true, correct, and complete. Declaration of preparer (other than taxpayer) is based on all information of which preparer has any knowledge.

Your signature	Date	Your occupation	Daytime telephone number (optional)
Spouse's signature. If a joint return, BOTH must sign.	Date	Spouse's occupation	( )

Paid Preparer's Use Only

Preparer's signature		Date	Check if self-employed ☐	Preparer's social security no.
Firm's name (or yours if self-employed) and address				EIN
				ZIP code

IRS Tax Court Cases, Revenue Rulings, and Letters

Uphus and Walker v. IRS Commissioner
Tax Court Memo 1994-71, February 23, 1994

Summary of the Decision

The U.S. Tax Court ruled that two providers could claim that their basement areas and garages were regularly used for their business, despite the fact that child care children only occasionally entered these spaces. The IRS position had been that providers were not entitled to claim any space in the home as regularly used for business unless child care children regularly played in the space. In rejecting this position, the Tax Court looked at how the items in the room (toys, supplies, washer, dryer, and so on) were used by the business and whether the provider used the room regularly: "The fact that the children were generally not allowed in the areas is not dispositive of the issue. The issue is whether the area in question is regularly used in the operation of the taxpayer's day-care business, not whether or not the children are present in that area."

In deciding the issue of whether the garages of the two providers were regularly used for the business, the Court ruled in favor of one provider (Uphus) and against the other provider (Walker). Tom Copeland handled the Tax Court appeal for the two providers.

Here is how the Court described the use of each garage in reaching its decision:

(Uphus): "The garage was used by Mrs. Uphus to park her car and store both day-care and Uphus personal items. Mr. Uphus' car was always parked on the street. The garage contained the majority of the outside day-care play items; i.e., scooter bikes, sandbox toys, wagons, a movable cardboard basketball hoop, a slide, etc. The garage was also used to store lawn chairs, lawn-care materials, tools, a snowblower, bicycles, and miscellaneous other items that were stored in the rafters.

"During an average day, Mrs. Uphus and the older children were constantly entering the garage to retrieve and return the outdoor play items; the young children were not allowed to enter the garage unsupervised. A few times a month, when Mrs. Uphus took the day-care children on field trips, i.e., to the library, zoo, and grocery store, the garage was used to access her car. During the winter, the Uphuses used the snowblower to clear their home entrance for the day-care children, and in the summer and spring, the Uphuses used the lawn-care materials to maintain the yard. Often, Mrs. Uphus used the tools in the garage to fix the bikes or other play items."

(Walker): "The Walker garage was rarely used in the day-care business. The children were prohibited from playing in the garage. The Walker garage generally contained Mrs. Walker's car and miscellaneous personal items of the Walkers. Mr. Walker's car was parked on the street. On occasion, one of the day-care children would leave a bicycle in the garage during the day. A few times a week, Mrs. Walker used the garage to access her car when she took the children on field trips, usually to the library, park, or zoo. Four days a week, the day-care children used the garage to access Mrs. Walker's car because she took the day-care children with her when she drove her child to preschool."

This case can help in clarifying several other issues:

1) Providers should count the square footage of their garage as part of the total square feet of their home. Most providers will be able to claim that they regularly use this space for their business.

2) Basement rooms may be considered regularly used for business even if they are off-limits to children because of licensing restrictions.

3) Providers who regularly use all of the rooms in their home for their business are entitled to claim 100 percent of their space as business use.

Robert Neilson and Dorothy Neilson v. Commissioner
Tax Court Decision 94-1, 1990

Respondent's Deficiency Determination

During 1983 and 1984 petitioners operated a licensed day-care center in their home. Petitioners purchased their 3,000-square-foot home in 1981 for $119,624, of which $75,285 was allocable to the house. Eighty-nine percent of the 3,000 square feet of space was utilized for day-care purposes. The following schedules reflect the amount of deductions claimed by petitioners and allowed by respondent for the 1983 and 1984 taxable years:

Respondent determined that petitioners' use of their residence for day-care services was 75 hours per week. Respondent's estimate was based upon a log kept by petitioners that reflects the times and days that children were in petitioners' care.

In addition to the time children were actually present in petitioners' residence, petitioners spend about 2 hours each morning organizing the facility and preparing luncheon meals for the children. Petitioners also spent about one hour each evening after the children departed cleaning and reorganizing the day-care facility. Respondent did not consider the preparation and clean-up time in estimating 75 hours per week. Petitioners, on occasion, also provided day care on weekends. Respondent's formula did not consider the weekend use of petitioners' residence. Petitioners utilized their residence for day-care business purposes for an average of 90 hours per week or 54 percent (90 ÷ 168) of the time.

Petitioners claimed and respondent disallowed $532 and $608 for lawn care in 1983 and 1984 respectively. During 1983 and 1984 petitioners used the lawn areas around their residence for day-care business purposes. During 1983 and 1984 petitioners paid $532 and $608, respectively for lawn care expenses, 54 percent of which is deductible in each taxable year.

Type of Deduction	Claimed in 1983	Allowed in 1983	Claimed in 1984	Allowed in 1984
Depreciation[2]	$5,057.00	$1,994.00	$5,057.00	$1,994.00
Lawn Care	532.00	- 0 -	608.00	- 0 -
Utilities	753.94	792.00	1,348.37	602.37
Repairs	960.00	442.90	- 0 -	- 0 -
Insurance	425.00	190.00	697.59	311.59
Real Estate Tax	1,369.44	611.44	1,464.29	654.29
Interest-Mtg.	5,455.17	3,171.17	7,035.85	3,912.86

[2]Petitioners claimed ACRS depreciation on the straight-line method for a 15-year useful life. Respondent determined that only 89 percent of the residence was used for day-care purposes and that day care was provided for only 75 out of a possible 168 hours per week, or 44.6 percent of the total time available for use. With the exception of the lawn care, which was disallowed completely, all other deductions were reduced to reflect the 89-percent and 75-hour factors determined by respondent.

Respondent concedes that any disallowed portion of real estate tax and interest would be deductible as "**Schedule A**" items. Petitioners concede that for 1983 the amount of interest claimed exceeded the amount they could verify and that they are therefore not entitled to $119 of the total deduction taken. Petitioners also concede that their personal use of the residence constituted 11 percent and, accordingly, only 89 percent can be considered for business purposes.

Income Tax Deficiency–Merits

Generally, under Section 280A, no deduction otherwise allowable shall be allowed with respect to the use of a dwelling unit which is used by a taxpayer as a residence during the taxable year. An exception to the general rule exists where the residence is used exclusively and on a regular basis as the principal place of business for any trade or business of the taxpayer. Sec. 280A(c)(1). Additionally, where a taxpayer uses a dwelling unit on a regular basis for day-care services, a deduction may be allowable based upon percentage of use. Section 280A(c)(4)(C) provides for a deduction in an amount equal to the expenses attributable to that portion determined by multiplying the total amount of the expense by a fraction, the numerator of which is the number of hours the portion is used for day care business purposes and the denominator of which is the total number of hours that the portion is available for use. Sec, 1.280-2(i)(4), Proposed Income Tax Regs., 45 Fed. Reg. 52399 (1980), amended 48 Fed Reg. 33320 (1983).

Petitioners bear the burden of proving the amount of their use and their entitlement to a deduction. *Welch v. Helvering*, 290 U.S. 111 (12 AFTR 1456) (1933); Rule 142(a). Initially, petitioners have conceded that 89 percent of their residence was utilized for day-care purposes and that 11 percent was used for personal use.

Petitioners maintained a log which reflected the name of the child, the date, and time spent at petitioners' residence. Respondent, based upon the log, determined that petitioners used their residence about 75 hours per week. Based upon petitioners' testimony, we have determined that petitioners used their residence about 90 hours per week. Our finding is based upon that preparation and clean-up time which is not reflected on petitioners' log and upon the fact that petitioners occasionally provided day-care service on weekends. Respondent's determination of 75 hours per week is apparently based upon a 5-day week and 15-hours use per day. With 90 in the numerator and 168 in the denominator, petitioners would be entitled to 54 percent of 89 percent of the items claimed on their returns in connection with day care, except for the lawn care. The 89 percent limit does not apply to the lawn care because it appears that the children had exclusive use of that area during the time day care was being provided. Accordingly, 54 percent of the $532 and $608 claimed for lawn care in 1983 and 1984 respectively is allowable.

Commission of Internal Revenue v. Soliman 91-998
Supreme Court of the United States
January 12, 1993

This significant case clarifies what factors should be used to determine whether a person may claim deductions for using their home for their business. The key issue in this case was whether or not the office in the taxpayer's home was the "principal place of business" for the taxpayer's business. In deciding the case against allowing the taxpayer to deduct home office expenses, the Court looked at the following:

a)   The relative importance of the functions performed at home versus other locations away from home, and

b)   The relative time spent at home versus other locations away from home.

The taxpayer lost because his home was not the point where his primary services were performed and because he spent more hours working away from home than he did at his home.

Impact on Family Child Care

Although this case is important for people using their home for business purposes, it does not affect family child care providers. Clearly, a provider's home is the principal place of business for doing child care. All the child care services are delivered from the home and the vast majority of time spent doing child care is spent in the home. Note: Some providers rent space in another building to do child care. Because of this case, a provider may have a harder time claiming home office expenses for her home in addition to claiming expenses for the rented building.

IRS Bulletin No. 92-29 April 20, 1992
Part I. Rulings and Decisions Under the Internal Revenue Code of 1986
Section 62.— Adjusted Gross Income Defined
26 CFR1.62-IT: Adjusted gross income. (Also Section 162; 1.162-1.)

Tax preparation expenses; deductibility. The Service has ruled that expenses incurred by an individual in preparing that portion of the taxpayer's return that relates to the taxpayer's business as a sole proprietor is deductible as a trade or business expense in determining the taxpayer's adjusted gross income under Section 62(a)(1) of the Code. Rev. Rul. 70-40 modified.

Rev. Rul. 92-29

Issue

Are the following expenses deductible as trade or business expenses in determining the taxpayer's adjusted gross income under section 62(a)(1) of the Internal Revenue Code: (1) expenses incurred by an individual taxpayer in preparing that portion of the taxpayer's return that relates to the taxpayer's business as a sole proprietor, and (2) expenses incurred in resolving to the taxpayer's business as a sole proprietor?

Facts

A, an individual taxpayer, operates a consulting business as a sole proprietorship. During 1992, A pays P, a tax return preparer, $500 to prepare A's federal income tax return. Of the $500, $200 is properly allocable to preparing Schedule C (Profit or Loss from Business). The remaining $300 is properly allocable to preparing the remainder of A's federal income tax return, including Form 1040, Schedule A (Interest and Dividend Income). During 1992, A also pays P $800 for services rendered in resolving asserted tax deficiencies relating to the business income of A's sole proprietorship.

Law and Analysis

Section 162(a) of the Code allows a deduction for all the ordinary and necessary expenses paid or incurred during the taxable year in carrying on any trade or business.

Section 62(a) of the Code provides that "adjusted gross income" means, in the case of an individual, gross income minus specified deductions. Under section 62(a)(1), one of the specified deductions is any deduction attributable to a trade or business carried on by the taxpayer, if that trade or business does not consist of the performance of services by the taxpayer as an employee.

Section 1.62-IT(d) of the temporary Income Tax Regulations provides, in part, that to be deductible in determining adjusted gross income, expenses must be those directly, and not those merely remotely, connected with the conduct of a trade or a business. As an example of the required relationship, the regulation states that property taxes paid or incurred on real property used in a trade or business are deductible in determining adjusted gross income.

The legislative history to the predecessor of section 62 of the Code states: Fundamentally, the deductions thus permitted to be made from gross income in arriving at adjusted gross income are those which are necessary to make as nearly equivalent as practicable the concept of adjusted gross income, when that concept is applied to different types of taxpayers deriving their income from varying sources... For example, in the case of an individual merchant or store proprietor, gross income under the law is gross receipts less the cost of goods sold; it is necessary to reduce this amount by the amount of business expenses before it becomes comparable...to the salary or wages of an employee in the usual case.

S. Rep. No. 885, 78th Cong., 2d Sess. 24-25 (1944), 1944 C.B. 858, at 877-78

Based on the purpose of section 62(a)(1) of the Code, the Service will allow the following expenses as deductions in determining the taxpayer's adjusted gross income under section 62(a)(1): (1) expenses incurred by an individual taxpayer in preparing that portion of the taxpayer's return that relates to the taxpayer's business as a sole proprietor; and (2) expenses incurred in resolving asserted tax deficiencies relating to the taxpayer's business as a sole proprietor.

In the present case, A, in determining adjusted gross income under section(a)(1) of the Code, may deduct the $200 expense for preparing Schedule C and the $800 expense for resolving asserted tax deficiencies relating to the business income of A's sole proprietorship. A may deduct the remaining $300 expense from adjusted gross income as an itemized deduction under section 212(3) in determining taxable income, subject to the 2 percent floor limitation under section 67.

Holding

The following expenses are deductible as trade or business expenses in determining the taxpayer's adjusted gross income under section 62(a)(1) of the Code: expenses incurred by an individual taxpayer in preparing that portion of the taxpayer's return that relates to the taxpayer's business as a sole proprietor, and expenses incurred in resolving asserted tax deficiencies relating to the taxpayer's business as a sole proprietor. Expenses incurred in preparing schedules or resolving asserted tax deficiencies relating to profit or loss from business (Schedule C), income or loss from rentals or royalties (Part I of Schedule E, Supplemental Income and Loss), or farm income and expenses (Schedule F), are deductible under section 62(a).

Effects on Other Documents

Rev. Rul. 70-40, 1970-1 C.B. 50, is modified to the extent that it holds that no deduction is allowed under section 62(a)(1) of the Code for litigating expenses incurred in determining state and federal income taxes on income derived from a trade or business carried on by the taxpayer.

Drafting Information

The principal author of this revenue ruling is G. Channing Horton of the Office of Assistant Chief Counsel (Income Tax and Accounting). For further information regarding this revenue ruling, contact Mr. Horton (202-566-3627).

IRS Bulletin No. 92-3 January 21, 1992
Part I. Rulings and Decisions Under the Internal Revenue Code of 1986
Section 262.-Personal, Living, and Family Expenses

If a taxpayer provides day care in the taxpayer's home, are the costs of basic local telephone service for the first telephone line provided to the home and other substantiated telephone charges deductible under section 262(b) of the Code? See Rev. Rul. 92-3, below.

Section 280A,-Disallowance of Certain Expenses in Connection with Business Use of a Home, Rental of Vacation Homes, etc.
(Also Section 262.)

Calculation of the deduction for the business use of a home by day care providers. A day care provider should compute the amount of the deduction by treating a room as used for day care for the entire business day if it is available for day care use for the entire day and is regularly used for day care.

Rev. Rul. 92-3

Issue

How should a day care provider compute the amount of the deduction provided under section 280A of the Internal Revenue Code for the business use of the provider's home for day care during a taxable year?

Facts

A, an individual, operates a full-time day care facility in A's home in state M. A is a licensed day care provider under the laws of M. A's day care business is regularly operated 11 hours each day (from 7 a.m. to 6 p.m.), 5 days a week, 250 days a year. During these business hours, A provides day care for several young children other than A's children. Some children arrive at A's home for day care at 7 a.m., and some do not leave A's home until 6 p.m. At any particular time during A's business day, A has at least 1 child (other than A's children) in A's home for day care.

The total floor area of A's home is 1,600 square feet. Although no rooms in A's home are used exclusively for A's day care business, several rooms in A's home are available for day care use throughout A's business day and are regularly so used as part of A's routine provision of day care. The total floor area of these rooms is 1,200 square feet. In addition, A spends one-half hour before and one-half hour after regular business hours preparing for and cleaning up after the children.

In addition to interest and taxes of $5,000, A, a calendar year taxpayer, incurred $4,000 of costs during 1991 for electricity, gas, water, trash collection, general maintenance, and insurance with respect to the use of A's home for day care and as a personal residence. The total depreciation for A's home during 1991 (determined under sections 167 and 168 as though the entire home were depreciable) was $1,000. Thus, A's total costs for 1991 were $10,000.

A's home has only one telephone line and A pays a monthly charge of $20 for basic local telephone service. The laws of M require A to have a telephone in order to be licensed by M to provide day care. A uses the telephone for both business and personal calls.

A has adequate records to substantiate the $10,000 of costs, the number of hours and days that A's day care business was operated (including preparation and clean-up time), the number of children for whom A provided day care, and A's telephone costs.

Law and Analysis

Section 280A(a) of the Code provides generally that in the case of a taxpayer who is an individual or an S corporation, no deduction otherwise allowable shall be allowed with respect to the use of a dwelling unit that is used by the taxpayer during the taxable year as a residence.

Under section 280A(b), subsection (a) shall not apply to any deduction otherwise allowable to the taxpayer without regard to the deduction's connection with the trade or business (for example, the deduction for qualified residence interest under section 163 and the deduction for state and local real property taxes on a personal residence under section 164).

Section 280A(c)(4)(A) of the Code provides, in part, that subsection (a) shall not apply to any item to the extent that the item is allocable to the use of any portion of the dwelling unit on a regular basis in the taxpayer's trade or business of providing day care.

Section 280A(c)(4)(B) of the Code provides, in part, that paragraph (a) shall apply only if the owner or operator of the trade or business has applied for, has been granted, or is exempt from having a license, certification, registration, or approval as a day care center or as a family or group day care home under the provisions of any applicable state law.

Section 280A(c)(4)(C) of the Code provides, in part, that if a portion of the taxpayer's dwelling used in the day care business is not used exclusively for day care purposes, the amount of expenses attributable to that portion shall not exceed an amount that bears the same ratio to the total amount of the items allocable to such portion as the number of hours that portion is used for such purposes bears to the number of hours the portion is available for use.

Section 280A(c)(5) of the Code, in part, limits the section 280A(c)(4) deduction for day care expenses to the excess of the gross income derived from the day care business over the otherwise allowable deductions allocable to the day care business (e.g., interest and taxes) and the deductions allocable to that business that are now allocable to the use of the dwelling (e.g., food and supplies).

Section 262(b) of the Code provides that, in the case of an individual, any charge for basic local telephone service with respect to the first telephone line provided to any residence of the taxpayer shall be treated as a nondeductible personal expense.

In computing the deduction for a taxable year under section 280A(c)(4) of the Code for the business use of A's home to provide day care, A should multiply the total costs incurred during the year with respect to A's home ($10,000) by two fractions. (If A rented rather than owned A's home, the amount of rent paid in 1991, rather than the depreciation, mortgage interest, and real estate taxes would be included in the costs incurred.) The first fraction is the total square footage in A's home that is available for day care used throughout each business day and that is regularly so used in that business, divided by the total square footage of A's home. The second fraction is the total hours in the year that the day care business is operated (including substantiated preparation and clean-up time), divided by the total number of hours in a year (8,760 hours). If a room is available for day care use throughout each business day and is regularly used as part of A's routine provision of day care (including a bathroom, an eating area for meals, or a bedroom used for naps), the square footage of that room will be considered as used for day care throughout each business day. A day care provider is not required to keep records of the specific hours of usage of such a room during business hours. Also, the occasional nonuse of such a room for a business day will not disqualify the room from being considered regularly used. However, the occasional use of a room that is ordinarily not available as part of the routine provision of day care (e.g., a bedroom ordinarily restricted from care use but used occasionally for naps) will not be considered as used for day care throughout each business day.

Thus, except as limited by section 280A(c)(5) of the Code, A may deduct under section 280A(c)(4) $2,568.49, which represents the portion of the $10,000 in expenses attributable to A's use of 1,200 square feet of A's home for day care for 3,000 hours (12 hours per day for 250 days) during 1991. The computation of the $2,568.49 day care deduction is as follows: (1200/1600) x (3000/8760) x $10,000 = $2,568.49. The nonbusiness portion of the otherwise deductible interest and taxes may be claimed as an itemized deduction.

Under section 262(b) of the Code, A's $20 monthly expense for basic local telephone service is a nondeductible personal expense, even though the state requires A to have a telephone in order to be a licensed day care provider. Additional telephone charges incurred for business purposes are deductible under section 162 to the extent substantiated.

Holding

A day care provider should compute the amount of the deduction for a taxable year provided under section 280A of the Code for the business use of a home for day care by multiplying the total costs incurred during the year that are allocable to the use of the home by two fractions. The first fraction is the total square footage in the home that is available for day care use throughout each business day and that is regularly so used in that business, divided by the total square footage of the home. The second fraction is the total hours in the year that the day care business is operated (including substantiated preparation and clean-up time), divided by the total number of hours in a year. This deduction is limited as provided in section 280A(c)(5).

In addition, pursuant to section 262(b), no deduction is allowed for the cost of basic local telephone service for the first telephone line provided to the home.

Drafting Information

The principal author of this revenue ruling is Cynthia A. Davis of the Office of Assistant Chief Counsel (Income Tax and Accounting). For further information regarding this revenue ruling, contact Ms. Davis (202-566-4177).

IRS Revenue Ruling 82-26

Section 1034.- Rollover of Gain on Sale of Principal Residence
26 CFR 1.1034-1: Sale or exchange of residence. (Also Section 280A.)

Residence; business use; limitations on deferral of gain. The part of the gain on the sale of a personal residence that is allocable to the part of the residence used in the taxpayer's trade or business may not be deferred under section 1034 of the Code if the business use met the requirements of section 280A(c)(1) in the year of sale. However, no allocation is required if the business use of a part of residence in the year of sale does not meet the requirements of section 280A(c)(1).

Issue

Under the circumstances described below, is gain recognized under section 1034 of the Internal Revenue Code on the sale of a principal residence when a part of the residence was used for business purposes?

Facts

Situation 1: In January 1976, A, a 39-year-old individual, purchased a used home for 70x dollars. This home was used as A's principal residence. A used a part of the home exclusively

Teaching Family Child Care Record Keeping and Tax Preparation

on a regular basis to see patients in connection with A's occupation as a doctor. With regard to such use, A claimed, and was allowed, in each taxable year a business deduction. In December 1981, A sold the home; the adjusted sale price was 120x dollars. Also in December 1981, A purchased for 140x dollars a new home. No part of the new home was used in connection with A's trade or business; that is, the home was used exclusively as a principal residence by A.

Situation 2: In 1970 B, a 39-year-old individual, purchased a used home for 40x dollars. This home was used as B's principal residence. B also used a part of the home for as an office in connection with B's occupation as a school teacher.

In connection with B's occupation, B claimed a deduction under section 162 of the Code with regard to an office in the home for the years 1971 through 1975. The deductions were allowed based on 25 percent use of the home for business purposes. However, for 1976 and subsequent years, deductions were not allowable because of section 280A, which became effective for taxable years beginning after December 31, 1975. However, B continued to use the home office in connection with B's business. In November 1981, B sold the home, and the adjusted sales price was 80x dollars. Also in November 1981, B purchased for 90x dollars a new home. That home was used exclusively by B as a principal residence, no part of which was used in connection with B's trade or business so as to qualify for deduction under section 280A(c)(1).

Law and Analysis

Section 1034 of the Code provides that if a taxpayer sells property (the "old residence") used by the taxpayer as a principal residence and, within a period beginning 2 years after such date, property (the "new residence") is purchased and used by the taxpayer as a principal residence, gain (if any) from such sale shall be recognized only to the extent that the taxpayer's adjusted sales price of the old residence exceeds the taxpayer's cost of purchasing the new residence. (Generally, for "old residences" sold or exchanged before January 20, 1980, the 2 year periods are 18 months.)

Section 1.1034-1(c)(3)(ii) of the Income Tax Regulations provides that where part of a property is used by the taxpayer as a principal residence and part is used for other purposes, an allocation must be made to determine the application of section 1034 of the Code. If the old residence is used only partially for residential purposes, only that part of the gain allocable to the residential portion is not to be recognized under section 1034. Also, only an amount allocable to the selling price of such portion need be reinvested in the new residence in order to have the gain allocable to such portion not recognized under section 1034.

Section 280A(a) of the Code provides that in the case of an individual taxpayer no deduction otherwise allowable shall be allowed with respect to the use of a dwelling unit that is used by the taxpayer during the taxable year as residence, except as otherwise provided in section 280A.

Section 280A(c)(1) of the Code provides that subsection (a) shall not apply to any item to the extent the item is allocable to a portion of the dwelling unit that is used exclusively on a regular basis (A) as the taxpayer's principal place of business; (B) as a place of business that is used by patients, clients, or customers in meeting or dealing with the taxpayer in a normal course of the taxpayer's trade or business; or (C) in the case of a separate structure that is not attached to the dwelling unit, in connection with the taxpayer's trade or business.

Rev. Rul. 59-72, 1959-1 C.B. 203. holds that where all the facts and circumstances indicate that property sold by a taxpayer was used by the taxpayer as a taxpayer's principal residence, the taxpayer will be entitled to relief provided for by section 1034 of the Code, notwithstanding the fact that the taxpayer temporarily rented out the residence prior to its sale. Thus, the Service looks to the use of the property at the time of sale.

When part of a property is used as a principal residence and part is used, until it is sold, for business, nonrecognition of gain under section 1034 of the Code is limited to the gain realized on the part of the property used as a residence. Although not every use of a principal residence in connection with a taxpayer's trade or business will limit the application of section 1034, when the taxpayer uses the residence in a trade or business in the manner and to the extent prescribed by section 280A(c)(1), there is a business use of a part of the property within the meaning of section 1.1034-1(c)(3)(ii) of the regulations. Thus any gain of the sale must be allocated between the business and residential parts of the property.

In Situation 1, a part of A's residence was used in connection with A's medical practice until it was sold. The part of the home that was used in connection with A's occupation as a doctor was used exclusively on a regular basis as an office in which A met with patients in the normal course of the medical practice. Thus, the requirements of section 280A(c)(1) of the Code were satisfied and deductions were allowed with respect to the business use of the residence. Because the criteria of section 280A(c)(1) were met, A must make the allocation required by section 1.1034-1(c)(3)(ii) of the regulations.

The fact that the taxpayer was allowed business expense deductions for the use of a residence prior to 1976 does not mean that an allocation is required under section 1.1034-1(c)(3)(ii) of the regulations. Not every use of a residence in connection with a taxpayer's trade or business necessitates an allocation. When such use does not meet the standards of section 280A(c)(1) of the Code, the taxpayer is not considered to have used a part of the property for business purposes within the meaning of section 1.1034-1(c)(3)(ii).

In Situation 2, for the taxable years 1971 through 1975, B was allowed deductions under section 162 of the Code for the part of the home used as an office in connection with B's occupation as a teacher. However, after the effective date of section 280A, section 162 deductions were not allowed to B for the part of the home used in connection with B's occupation as a teacher, and B's use of the residence did not meet the standards of section 280A(c)(1) of the Code.

Holding

In Situation 1, A must make the allocation required under section 1.1034(c)(3)(ii) of the regulations, and may defer under section 1034 of the Code only that part of the gain on the sale of the residence that is allocable to the residential portion of the property.

In Situation 2, B is not required to make any allocation of the gain on the sale if the residence under section 1.1034-1(c)(3)(ii) of the regulations and may defer under section 1034 of the Code the entire gain on the sale of the residence.

IRS Revenue Ruling 79-142

Issue

What are the federal income tax consequences to family and group day care home operators who participate in the Child Care Food Program (CCF program) authorized by the National School Lunch Act and Child Nutrition Act of 1966 Amendments of 1975, Pub. L. No. 94-105, 94th Cong., 1st Sess. (October 7, 1975), 42 U.S.C. Section 1766 (Supp. V 1976)?

Facts

Situation 1: Under the auspices of a sponsoring charitable organization described in section 170(c) of the Code, which was formed to provide day care and nutritional meals to needy children, an individual operates a nonprofit licensed day care service in the individual's home and provides meals at lunch time to the children cared for. Pursuant to the CCF program administered by the Department of Agriculture, the sponsoring organization has entered into an agreement with the State Department of Education whereby the organization has agreed to accept final financial and administrative responsibility for the conduct of the food service provided in the day care home under its authority. In the agreement the sponsoring organization ensures the state agency that meals served in the individual's day care home meet specified requirements, and that meals are served free or at a reduced price to all children eligible for free and reduced price meals under the CCF program. The sponsoring organization is also required (1) to provide consultation and technical assistance to ensure that meals meet prescribed standards, that adequate records are maintained, and that other CCF program requirements are met, (2) to train day care personnel responsible for the food service, and (3) to make periodic visits to the day care home to monitor compliance.

In exchange, the state agency reimburses the sponsoring organization for the expenses incurred by the day care home operator in providing free and reduced price lunches to eligible children. The amount of the reimbursement payments is determined by the number and types of meals served and the need of the children enrolled in the CCF program. In no event may reimbursement payments to the sponsoring organization exceed the operating costs of the day care food service.

After receiving reimbursement payments from the state agency, the sponsoring organization distributes the funds to the individual operating the day care food service. In the taxable year in question, the payments made to the day care home operator are equal to the operating costs of the CCF program. No payments are made to the operator for the value of services rendered in preparing and dispensing the lunches.

Situation 2: An individual operates a day care service in the individual's home and provides lunches to needy children under the same facts as in Situation 1, except that in the taxable year in question the individual receives payments from the sponsoring organization that include not only reimbursements for operating expenses, but also payments for the value of the individual's services.

Law and Analysis

Section 61(a) of the Internal Revenue Code of 1954 provides that, except as otherwise provided by law, gross income means all income from whatever source derived. Section 162 (a) provides that there shall be allowed as a deduction all the ordinary and necessary expenses paid or incurred during the taxable year in carrying on a trade or business. Section 170 provides that, subject to certain limitations, a deduction shall be allowed for any charitable contribution(as defined in Section 170(c)) payment of which is made within the taxable year. Section 1.170A-1(g) of the Income Tax Regulations provides, in part, that reimbursed out-of-pocket expenditures made incident to the rendition of services to a charitable organization may constitute a deductible contribution.

Section 9(d) of the National School Lunch Act and Child Nutrition Act of 1966 Amendments of 1975 provides that "[t]he value of assistance to children under this Act shall not be considered to be income or resources for any purpose under any Federal or State laws, including laws relating to taxation and welfare and public assistance." Pursuant to section 9(d) of the Amendments of 1075, the value of free and reduced meals served to needy children under the CCF program is not includible in the gross incomes of the children or of their parents. However, reimbursements and payments received by operators of family and group day care homes under the CCF program are not excludable from their gross incomes for federal income tax purposes by reason of section 9(d) of the Amendments of 1975, but they may be otherwise excludable from the day care home operator's gross income depending on the particular facts.

The individual operating the day care home in Situation 1 does not have a profit making motive in operating the day care facility and is not, in fact, making a profit. The expenses incurred by the individual in Situation 1 in gratuitous services to the sponsoring organization. See Rev. Rul. 77-279 furtherance of the CCF program are incurred on behalf of the sponsoring charitable organization and are directly connected with the rendition of (Situation 1), 1977-2 C.B. 12.

In contrast, the individual operating the day care home in Situation 2 does have a profit motive and, in fact, received compensation for services rendered in connection with the lunches provided under the CCF program. Nevertheless, as in Situation 1, the food service expenditures subject to reimbursement were incurred by the individual in Situation 2 on behalf of the sponsoring organization. See Rev. Rul. 77-280 (Situations 3 and 4), 1977-2 C.B. 14.

Holdings

The payments received from the sponsoring organization in Situation 1 are not includible in the gross income of the individual as long as the payments do not exceed the expenses incurred by the individual in feeding the children eligible for assistance under the program.

The portion of each payment received by the individual in Situation 2 from the sponsoring organization that represents reimbursement of actual expenditures incurred on behalf of the sponsoring organization is not includible in the gross income of the individual. The portion of the payment attributable to compensation for the value of the individual's services is includible in the individual's gross income.

In both Situations 1 and 2, the individual's reimbursed expenditures are not the individual's own expenses, but are incurred on behalf of the sponsoring organization. Therefore, the reimbursed expenses are not deductible by the individual in either Situation 1 under section 170 of the Code or Situation 2 under section 162.

If in Situation 1 the operating costs of the CCF program had been greater than the reimbursement payments, the excess of the out-of-pocket expenses over the reimbursement would have been deductible by the individual within the limitations of section 170 of the Code as contributions for the use of the sponsoring organization, because the individual would be rendering gratuitous services to the sponsoring organization by feeding the children. See Rev. Rul. 77-280 (Situations 1 and 2).

If in Situation 2 the operating costs of the CCF program had been greater than the reimbursement payments, the excess of the out-of-pocket expenses over the reimbursement would have been deductible as a trade or business expenses under section 162 of the Code. See Rev. Rul. 77-280 (Situations 3 and 4).

IRS Letter to Minnesota Senator Rudy Boschwitz

Notes on the following February 6, 1990, letter from the IRS:

This IRS letter was written in response to a letter from former Minnesota Senator Rudy Boschwitz, who asked for a clarification on seven issues facing family child care providers.

Issue One: This letter clearly indicates that providers may count hours spent cooking, cleaning, and preparing activities for their business as part of their Time-Space calculation.

Issue Two: This letter indicates that whether a trip is primarily business or personal depends on the facts and circumstances of each case. Notice, however, that a trip can have some personal activity and still be considered a business trip. Some IRS auditors have said that if a trip has any personal activity, it cannot be claimed as a business trip. This is not true.

Issue Three: A provider who does not make a profit in three out of five years will not automatically be determined to not be in the business for profit.

Issue Four: The IRS is looking much more closely at Form 2441 to see if child care expenses and income match. A parent may not claim a child care tax credit if the provider is a dependent care center and does not comply with all state and local laws. A dependent care center is defined as someone caring for more than six children (not counting the provider's own children). In other words, a provider caring for six children or less can be illegal, according to local law, and the parent using this provider can claim the child care tax credit.

Issue Five: This letter does not answer the question of whether or not Child and Adult Care Food Program sponsors must issue Form 1099 to their providers. Currently, the IRS is not requiring this.

Issue Six: Capital expenses incurred to comply with licensing requirements must be depreciated and cannot be expensed in one year. If the expense is for personal property (i.e. fire extinguisher) and the business-use percent is over 50 percent, the item may be claimed as an expense in one year under Section 179 rules.

Issue Seven: The monthly base charge of a telephone is not deductible, even for a provider who is required to have a phone.

DEPARTMENT OF THE TREASURY
INTERNAL REVENUE SERVICE
WASHINGTON, D.C. 20224

OFFICE OF
CHIEF COUNSEL

FEB - 6 1990

The Honorable Rudy Boschwitz
United States Senate
Washington, D.C. 20510

Dear Senator Boschwitz:

This is in reference to your letter dated December 15, 1989, in which you ask a number of questions regarding the tax consequences under the Internal Revenue Code to child care providers, to taxpayers using the services of child care providers, and to food program sponsors.

Your first question concerns the deductibility of expenses for the business use of a home for providers of day care. Specifically, you ask whether hours spent cooking, cleaning, and preparing activities for the business of child care may be included in the calculation of the time-space percentage.

Section 162 of the Code provides, in general, that a deduction is allowed for the ordinary and necessary expenses paid or incurred during the taxable year in carrying on a trade or business. Whether an expense is ordinary and necessary and whether an expense is incurred in the conduct of a trade or business is largely a question of fact.

Section 262 states, that except as otherwise expressly provided, no deduction shall be allowed for personal, living, or family expenses.

Section 280A(a) of the Code states, in general, that except as otherwise provided, in the case of an individual, no deduction otherwise allowable shall be allowed with respect to the use of a dwelling unit that is used by the taxpayer during the year as a residence. Section 280A(c)(4)(A) provides, in part, that subsection (a) shall not apply to any item to the extent that the item is allocable to the use of any portion of the dwelling unit on a regular basis in the taxpayer's trade or business of providing day care for children.

Section 280A(c)(4)(C) of the Code indicates that if a portion of the taxpayer's dwelling unit is not used exclusively for child care, the amount of the expenses attributable to that portion of the dwelling shall not exceed an amount that bears the same ratio to the total amount allocable to such portion as the number of hours the portion is used for such purposes bears to

The Honorable Rudy Boschwitz

the number of hours available for use. This time-space percentage limits the amount of the deduction available to taxpayers based on the number of hours the dwelling is used exclusively for child care and the number of hours it is available for other use. A copy of Publication 587, Business Use of Your Home, is enclosed for your information.

Hours spent cooking, cleaning, and preparing activities for the business of child care could be included in the calculation of the time-space percentage if the tests for deduction under section 162 of the Code are otherwise met under the facts of the particular case. For instance, if a child care provider spends one-half hour setting up for the children and one-half hour returning a room to personal use, in addition to seven hours actually in the presence of the children, a provider could claim that eight hours were expended in the trade or business of providing day care for children.

As with any business use of a home, care providers must substantiate claims for hours expended in the conduct of the trade or business of providing child care. Publication 552, Recordkeeping for Individuals, and Publication 583, Taxpayers Starting a Business, provide information for taxpayers on how to keep adequate books and records for tax purposes. We have enclosed both publications for your information.

Section 6001 of the Code provides that every person liable for any tax shall keep records as prescribed by the Secretary of the Treasury. Section 1.6001-1(a) of the Income Tax Regulations provides that every person subject to income tax shall keep permanent books of accounts or records as are sufficient to establish the amount of gross income, deductions, credits, or other matters.

Your second question concerns the business use of a car by child care providers. Specifically, how many miles may be deducted when a provider drives to a store to buy items for both business and personal use.

Section 1.162-1 of the regulations provides that business expenses deductible from gross income include operating expenses of automobiles used in a trade or business. Section 1.162-2(b) provides that if a taxpayer travels to a destination and engages in both personal and business activities, traveling expenses to and from such destination are deductible only if the trip is related primarily to the taxpayer's trade or business. If the trip is primarily personal in nature, the traveling expenses to and from the destination are not deductible even though the

The Honorable Rudy Boschwitz

taxpayer engages in business while at such destination. Whether a trip is related primarily to the taxpayer's trade or business or is primarily personal in nature depends on the facts and circumstances in each case. The amount of time during the period of the trip that is spent on personal activity compared to the amount of time spent on activities directly relating to the taxpayer's trade or business is an important factor in determining whether the trip is primarily personal.

If an automobile trip is primarily for business, a taxpayer may deduct actual expenses or use the standard mileage rate, depending on the facts and circumstances. The enclosed Publication 917, Business Use of a Car, explains the deductible expenses. This publication also discusses what records must be kept to substantiate vehicle expenses, including the cost or other basis of the vehicle and the number of personal and business miles driven during the year.

Your third question concerns whether a child care provider is considered to be engaged in an activity for profit. Specifically, you question whether a child care provider who does not show a profit in three of five years automatically becomes classified as not in the business for profit and therefore becomes ineligible for business deductions.

Section 183 of the Code provides, in the case of an individual, if an activity is not engaged in for profit, no deduction attributable to the activity shall be allowed except as provided. Section 183(d) establishes a presumption that if gross income exceeds the deductions for an activity in three of five consecutive taxable years, the activity shall be considered engaged in for profit.

Section 1.183-1 of the regulations provides that whether an activity is engaged in for profit is determined under section 162 of the Code and section 212(1) and (2) except insofar as section 183(d) creates a presumption that the activity is engaged in for profit. If deductions are not allowable under sections 162 and 212(1) and (2), the deduction allowance rules of section 183(b) and the regulations apply.

Section 1.183-2(a) of the regulations defines the term "activity not engaged in for profit" as any activity other than one with respect to which deductions are allowable under section 162 of the Code or under paragraph (1) or (2) of section 212. The determination of whether an activity is engaged in for profit is to be made by reference to objective standards, taking into account all of the facts and circumstances of each case.

The Honorable Rudy Boschwitz

Section 1.183-2(b) of the regulations provides that in determining whether an activity is engaged in for profit, no one factor is determinative. The section lists objective factors that should normally be considered, including the manner in which the taxpayer carries on the activity, the expertise of the taxpayer or his advisors, the time and effort expended by the taxpayer in carrying on the activity, and the taxpayer's history of income or losses with respect to the activity. Section 1.183-2(b)(1) states that the fact that the taxpayer carries on the activity in a businesslike manner and maintains complete and accurate books and records may indicate that the activity is engaged in for profit.

Since section 183(d) merely establishes a presumption that favors the taxpayer if income exceeds deductions in three of five years, a child care provider who does not show a profit in three out of five years will not automatically be determined to not be in the business for profit.

Your fourth question refers to the credit available to taxpayers using the services of child care providers under section 21 of the Code for expenses incurred for child and dependent care. Specifically, you ask whether parents may claim the child care credit if they use a child care provider who does not meet state and local standards.

Section 21 of the Code provides, in part, that an individual who maintains a household that includes one or more qualifying individuals shall be allowed as a credit an amount equal to the applicable percentage of the employment-related expenses paid during the tax year. The amount of credit is subject to both dollar and earned income limitations. Section 21(e) outlines special rules for taking the child and dependent care credit.

If the service provider is a dependent care center as defined in section 21(b)(2)(D), payments made to such a care provider shall only be taken into account for purposes of the credit if the center complies with all applicable laws and regulations of a state or local government. Thus, parents may not claim a credit for payments made to a dependent care center unless the center complies with all applicable laws and regulations of state and local governments.

There is currently no requirement that other care providers comply with applicable state and local standards before a parent may claim the credit for expenses paid to the care provider. However, a care provider who does not comply with the provisions

The Honorable Rudy Boschwitz

of applicable state laws will be ineligible for a deduction under section 280A(c)(4)(B) of the Code for business use of a home.

Beginning in 1989, taxpayers claiming a credit under section 21 of the Code must include on their tax return the name, address, and taxpayer identification number of the child care provider. A copy of Publication 503, Child and Dependent Care Expenses, is enclosed for your information.

Your fifth question concerns information reporting requirements of sponsors of the Child Care Food Program. Specifically, you question whether food program sponsors are required to issue Forms 1099 to participating child care providers.

To assist the Internal Revenue Service in ascertaining whether taxpayers have correctly calculated their tax liabilities, the law requires certain persons to file information returns. Generally, these information returns are required to be filed by persons who make payments to others in the course of their trade or business. The information returns filed with the Service are matched with the payees' income tax returns to detect the nonfiling or underreporting of income.

Section 6041 of the Code provides, in part, that all persons engaged in a trade or business making payments to another person of $600 or more in a taxable year are required to make information returns regarding the payments as prescribed by the Income Tax Regulations. Section 6041A requires a recipient of services to report payments made to a provider of services if the remuneration in a calendar year is $600 or more. The information return used to report such payments is Form 1099-MISC, Statement for Recipients of Miscellaneous Income.

Whether a particular food program sponsor must file a Form 1099 depends on whether the section 6041 tests, and particularly the trade or business test, are met in that case.

Your sixth question asks if a care provider is required by state or local law to modify the home to become licensed or certified, are these modifications repairs or improvements. This question concerns whether expenses incurred in modifying a residence to comply with licensing requirements are capital or deductible expenses.

Section 262(a) of the Code states, in part, that except as otherwise provided, no deduction shall be allowed for personal, living, or family expenses. Section 263 disallows a deduction for capital expenditures. A capital expenditure includes any

The Honorable Rudy Boschwitz

amount paid for permanent improvements or betterments that extend beyond the tax year made to increase the value of a property or estate.

Section 1.263(a)-1(b) provides, in part, that the disallowance for amounts paid for betterments or improvements include amounts expended to adapt property to a new or different use. In RKO Theaters, Inc. v. U.S., 163 F. Supp. 598 (Ct. Cl. 1958), a theater corporation was required to construct new exit facilities and fire escapes as a condition to the granting of a future license. The court held that even though the changes did not prolong the life of the theater or increase its value, the expenses were nevertheless permanent capital improvements and the expenditures had to be capitalized.

Although a capital expenditure may not be deducted, a taxpayer may be able to recover this cost by taking annual deductions for depreciation. We have enclosed Publication 534, Depreciation, for your information.

Your final question concerns the deductibility of telephone expenses. Specifically, is any portion of the monthly base charge of a telephone deductible if child care providers are required by law to have a telephone. Section 262(b) of the Code provides, in the case of an individual, that any charge for basic local telephone service with respect to the first telephone line provided to any residence of the taxpayer shall be treated as a personal expense. Section 262(a) provides that a personal expense is not deductible.

In a November 13, 1989, meeting with members of your staff, these and other questions we discussed in detail. It was agreed that many of your constituents have been misinformed as to the deductions available to, and the responsibilities required of, child care providers in your state. We have enclosed a copy of Publication 1224, Free IRS Community Outreach Tax Assistance, for your information.

The Community outreach program, which is one of the Internal Revenue Service's volunteer and education programs, is managed by the Taxpayer Service Division. Under this program, Service employees or trained volunteers conduct tax education seminars on a variety of topics for groups of individuals with common tax interests and provide group self-help tax return preparation.

During fiscal year 1989, the St. Paul District conducted nine tax education seminars on dependent care providers. These seminars were attended by 344 individuals. Additional seminars

The Honorable Rudy Boschwitz

addressing the topic are scheduled for 1990. For specific information on the times and places for these seminars or if you would like to discuss scheduling a seminar, we invite you contact the Taxpayer Education Coordinator in the St. Paul District by calling the number or writing to the address shown in Publication 1224.

We hope the information provided is of help to you. If we can be of further assistance in this matter, please contact Cynthia Davis of this office at 566-4177.

Sincerely,

EARNEST L. KENNEDY
Acting Assistant Chief Counsel
(Income Tax & Accounting)

IRS Publications

Publication 587 Business Use of Your Home (1997 Version)

Introduction

The term *home* includes a house, apartment, condominium, mobile home, or boat. It also includes structures on the property, such as an unattached garage, studio, barn, or greenhouse. However, it does not include any part of your property used exclusively as a hotel or inn.

Day-Care Facility

To deduct business expenses for a child care facility in your home, you must meet the test discussed earlier under "Qualifying for a Deduction," except that:

- You must meet child care licensing requirements,

- You do not have to use the space exclusively for child care, and

- If an area is not used exclusively for child care, you must reduce any expenses by the percentage of time the area is not available for business use.

What is a child care facility? To deduct expenses for using part of your home to provide child care services, you must meet the following requirements.

1) You must be in the trade or business of providing day care for children, for persons 65 or older, or for persons who are physically or mentally unable to care for themselves.

2) You must have applied for, been granted, or be exempt from having a license, certification, registration, or approval as a day-care center or as a family or group day-care home under applicable state law. You do not meet this requirement if your application was rejected or your license or other authorization was revoked.

Figuring the Deduction. If you regularly use part of your home for day care, figure what part of your home is used for day care, as explained earlier under Business Percentage. If you use that part exclusively for day care, deduct all the allocable expenses, subject to the deduction limit, as explained earlier.

If the use of part of your home as a day care facility is regular, but **not** exclusive, you must figure what part of available time you actually use it for business. A room that is available for use throughout each business day and that you regularly use in your business is considered to be used for day care throughout each business day. You do not have to keep records to show the specific hours the area was used for business. You may use the area occasionally for personal reasons. However, a room you use only occasionally for business does not qualify for the deduction.

To find what part of the available time you actually use your home for business, compare the total business-use time to the total time that part of your home can be used for all purposes. You may compare the hours of business use in a week with the number of hours in a week (168). Or you may compare the hours of business use for the tax year with the number of hours in your tax year (8,760 in 1997).

Example 1. In 1995, Mary Lake uses her basement to operate a day-care business for children. Her home totals 3,200 square feet. The basement is 1,600 square feet, or 50 percent of the total area of the home (1,600 ÷ 3,200). She uses the basement for day care an average of 12 hours a day, 5 days a week, for 50 weeks. During the other 12 hours, the family can use the basement. During the year, the basement is used for day care for a total of 3,000 hours (250 days x 12 hours). The basement can be used 8,760 hours (24 hours x 365 days) during the year. Only 34.25 percent (3,000 ÷ 8,760) of the expenses of her basement are business expenses. Mary may deduct 34.25 percent of any **direct expenses** for the basement. However, only 34.25 percent of the basement part of her **indirect expenses** are business expenses. Because the basement is 50 percent of the total area of her home, she can deduct 17.13 percent (50% of 34.25%) of her indirect expenses.

Mary completes Part I of **Form 8829** as shown in Figure B.

Figure B

Form **8829**	**Expenses for Business Use of Your Home**	OMB No. 1545-1266
Department of the Treasury Internal Revenue Service	▶ File only with Schedule C (Form 1040). Use a separate Form 8829 for each home you used for business during the year. ▶ See separate instructions.	19**97** Attachment Sequence No. **66**

Name(s) of proprietor(s)	Your social security number
Mary Lake	412 : 00 : 1234

Part I   Part of Your Home Used for Business

1	Area used regularly and exclusively for business, regularly for day care, or for storage of inventory or product samples. See instructions	**1**	1,600
2	Total area of home	**2**	3,200
3	Divide line 1 by line 2. Enter the result as a percentage	**3**	50 %

● For day-care facilities not used exclusively for business, also complete lines 4–6.
● All others, skip lines 4–6 and enter the amount from line 3 on line 7.

4	Multiply days used for day care during year by hours used per day	**4**	3,000 hr.	
5	Total hours available for use during the year (365 days × 24 hours). See instructions	**5**	8,760 hr.	
6	Divide line 4 by line 5. Enter the result as a decimal amount . . .	**6**	.3425	
7	Business percentage. For day-care facilities not used exclusively for business, multiply line 6 by line 3 (enter the result as a percentage). All others, enter the amount from line 3 . . . . . ▶	**7**		17.13 %

Example 2. Assume the same facts as in Example 1, except that Mary also has another room that is available each business day for children to take naps in. Although she did not keep a record of the number of hours the room was actually used for naps, it was used for part of each business day. Since the room was available during regular operating hours each business day and was used regularly in the business, it is considered to be used for day care throughout each business day. In figuring her expenses, 34.25 percent of any direct expenses of the basement and room are deductible. In addition, 34.25 percent of the indirect expenses of the basement and room are business expenses. Because the basement and room are 60 percent of the total area of her home, Mary can deduct 20.55 percent (60% of 34.25%) of her indirect expenses.

Meals. If you provide food for your day-care business, do not include the expense as a cost of using your home for business. Claim it as a separate deduction on your **Schedule C (Form 1040)**. You can deduct as a business expense 100 percent of the cost of food consumed by your day-care recipients and 50 percent of the cost of food consumed by your employees. But you can never deduct the cost of food consumed by you or your family.

If you deduct the cost of food for your day-care business, keep a separate record (with receipts) of your family's food costs.

Reimbursements you receive from a sponsor under the Child and Adult Food Care Program of the Department of Agriculture are only taxable to the extent they exceed your expenses for food for eligible children. If your reimbursements are more than your expenses for food, show the difference as income in Part 1 of **Schedule C**. If your food expenses are greater than the reimbursements, show the difference as an expense in Part V of **Schedule C**. Do not include payments or expenses for your own children if they are eligible for the program. Follow this procedure even if you receive a **Form 1099** reporting a payment from the sponsor.

Publication 534 Depreciation

Basis of Assets

Decrease the basis of your property by the depreciation you could have deducted on your tax returns under the method of depreciation you selected. If you took less depreciation than you could have under the method you selected, decrease the basis by the amount you could have taken under that method. If you did not take a depreciation deduction, then make the adjustments to basis for depreciation you could have taken. If you deducted more depreciation than you should have, decrease your basis as follows. Decrease it by an amount equal to the depreciation you should have deducted, as well as by the part of the excess depreciation you deducted that actually reduced your tax liability for any year.

In decreasing your basis for depreciation, take into account the amount deducted on your tax returns as depreciation, and any depreciation you must capitalize under the uniform capitalization rules.

For information on figuring the depreciation you should have claimed, see **Publication 946 How To Depreciate Property**.

Publication 917 Business Use of a Car (1997 Version)

Standard Mileage Rate

Interest. If you are an employee, you cannot deduct any interest paid on a vehicle loan. This applies even if you use the vehicle 100 percent for business as an employee. However, if you are self-employed and use your vehicle in your business, you can deduct that part of the interest expense that represents your business use of the vehicle. For example, if you use your vehicle 50 percent for business, you can deduct 50 percent of the interest on **Schedule C (Form 1040)**. You cannot deduct the rest of the interest expense.

Personal property taxes. If you itemize your deductions on **Schedule A (Form 1040)**, you can deduct on line 7 state and local personal property taxes on motor vehicles. You can take this deduction even if you use the standard mileage rate or if you do not use the vehicle for business.

If you are self-employed and use your vehicle in your business, you can deduct the business part of state and local personal property taxes on motor vehicles on **Schedule C, Schedule C-EZ, or Schedule F (Form 1040)**.

Parking fees and tolls. In addition to using the standard mileage rate, you can deduct any business-related parking fees and tolls. (Parking fees that you pay to park your vehicle at your place of work are nondeductible commuting expenses.)

Common Law Employee (Internal Revenue Code Section 3121(d)(2))

Common law employee status is determined by applying 20 factors to a particular case to determine whether an employer/employee relationship exists. Such relationship exists if the person for whom the worker performs services has the right to direct and control the worker in performing the services.

20 Common Law Factors

Employee	vs.	Independent Contractor
INSTRUCTIONS Complies with instructions about when, where and how work is to be performed.		Works his or her own schedule. Does the job his or her own way.
TRAINING Trained by an experienced employee working with him or her. Required to take correspondence courses. Required attendance at meetings and by other methods indicates that the employer wants the services performed in a particular method.		Uses his or her own methods and receives no training from the purchaser.
INTEGRATION Services of the individual are merged into the business. Success and continuation of the business depends upon these services. Employer coordinates work with that of other workers.		Success and continuation of business aren't dependent on his or her services.
SERVICES RENDERED PERSONALLY Services must be rendered personally. Not able to engage other people to do the work.		Contractor able to assign one of his or her people to do the job.
HIRING, SUPERVISING, AND PAYING ASSISTANTS Hires, supervises and pays workers at the direction of the employer (acts as foreman or representative of the employer).		Hires, supervises, and pays the other workers as the result of a contract under which he or she agreed to provide materials and labor and is responsible for the results.
CONTINUING RELATIONSHIP The individual continues to work for the same person year after year.		Hires to do one job. No continuous relationship.
SET HOUR OF WORK The hours and days are set by the employer.		Is master of his or her own time.
FULL TIME REQUIRED Must devote full time to the business of the employer. Restricts him or her from doing other gainful work.		Free to work when and for whom he or she chooses.
DOING WORK ON EMPLOYER'S PREMISES Implies that the employer has control, is physically within the employer's direction and supervision.		Works off employer's premise, uses own office, desk and telephone.

Teaching Family Child Care Record Keeping and Tax Preparation

Employee	vs.	Independent Contractor

ORDER AND SEQUENCE SET

Performs services in the order or sequence set by the employer. Service performed at his or her own pace.
Salesperson reports at the office at specific times, follows up on leads and performs certain tasks at certain times.

Salesperson works own schedule and usually has own office.

ORAL OR WRITTEN REPORTS

Required to submit regular oral or written reports to the employer.

Submits no reports.

PAYMENT BY HOUR, WEEK, MONTH

Paid by the employer of regular amounts at stated intervals.

Paid by the job on a straight commission.

FURNISHING OF TOOLS, MATERIAL

Employer furnishes tools, materials, etc.

Furnishes his or her own tools.

SIGNIFICANT INVESTMENT

Has a lack of investment and depends on the employer for such facilities.

Has real, essential, and adequate investment.

REALIZATION OF PROFIT OR LOSS

Cannot realize a profit or loss by making good or bad decisions.

Can realize a profit or suffer a loss as a result of his or her services.

WORKING FOR MORE THAN ONE FIRM AT A TIME

Usually works for one employer.

Works for a number of persons or firms at the same time.

MAKING SERVICE AVAILABLE TO GENERAL PUBLIC

Does not make his or her services available except through some company or business he or she does not have an interest in.

Has own office and assistants. Holds business license, listed in business directories or maintains business telephone. Advertises in newspaper.

RIGHT TO DISCHARGE

Can be discharged at anytime.

Cannot be fired so long as he or she produces a result which meets contract specifications.

RIGHT TO TERMINATE

Can end his or her relationship with employer at anytime.

Agrees to complete a specific job. Is responsible for its satisfactory completion or is legally obligated to make good.

Articles

Will Your Center Get a Bonus This Year?
How to Raise Your Income without Raising Your Rates
by Tom Copeland, JD

—Originally published in *Child Care Information Exchange,* **November 1993**

Is your center working closely with parents to get the maximum tax benefits from employer-provided dependent care plans? Across the country, an increasing number of parents have been surprising their child care center by giving them a "bonus." Money for this "bonus" has come from dependent care plans.

More and more employers are offering a benefit plan that allows employees to designate some of their wages to pay for child care expenses before these wages are subject to any taxes. Such plans are called by various names: dependent care plan, pre-tax spending account, flexible benefit plan, or salary reduction plan.

By participating in such plans, parents lower their taxable income and pay less in taxes. Employers also benefit by paying less in Social Security and Medicare taxes on the lower taxable income. These plans are different from the federal child care tax credit. In general, parents earning less than $20,000 are better off using the child care tax credit rather than participating in a dependent care plan. Parents using a dependent care plan may set aside up to $5,000 (pre-tax) per year for child care expenses. Such parents can usually save hundreds of dollars more than if they claimed the child care tax credit. For example, a parent earning over $30,000 a year and spending $4,000 on child care would save about $480 in federal taxes using the tax credit, whereas the same parent using a dependent care plan would save about $840.

Potential "Bonus" Opportunity

Parents who don't spend all of the money they set aside each year under a dependent care plan must return any unspent money to their employer. Centers should try to make sure that this doesn't happen by telling parents to give their program all of the money that was set aside in their plan. Parents may do this by paying an extra amount each week until the end of the year, or they may make a lump sum payment after the year is over. Parents may submit child care receipts to their employer plan up to 90 days after the end of the plan year (usually this means December 31). In other words, if a parent has $200 in unspent funds in his or her plan on December 31, 1993, the parent may still submit another receipt to your center for 1993 child care expenses up until March 31, 1994.

Working with Parents

Some parents may not realize they have not spent all of the money set aside in dependent care plans. Other parents may not understand that they can still give the money to the child care program, even after the year is over. Parents may not carry over any unspent money to the next year. This is against the law.

By the end of the year, most parents probably will not have any unspent money in their plans. But for those who do, there is no reason why your center shouldn't ask for it. Here are some tips on how to go about this:

- Encourage all parents to participate in employer-provided dependent care plans if their employer offers one. It's an easy way for parents to reduce their taxes.

Teaching Family Child Care Record Keeping and Tax Preparation

- Find out which parents are using such plans. One sure sign of this is if parents ask for a receipt every time they pay. However, not all employers demand that parents show them regular receipts. At the end of the year, give parents a notice indicating how much money they have spent on child care services (see sample notice).

Notice to Parents about Employer-Provided Dependent Care Plans

As of December 31, 1993, the _____ family has paid $_____ in 1993 for child care services from our child care program. Parents who participate in an employer-provided dependent care plan should be aware that they will forfeit any money they set aside in such a plan, if it is not spent by the end of the plan year.

If your family set aside more than the amount identified above for child care expenses in 1993, you may want to take steps to make sure that you spend all of the funds in your plan in a timely manner. Parents have until 90 days after the end of their plan year to submit receipts for child care expenses for 1993. Plan years usually end on December 31, 1993.

Remember that any money in your plan that is not spent on child care services will automatically be turned over to your employer. Child care funds may not be carried forward from one plan year to the next.

This is your opportunity to turn any unspent money over to our program. We will use this money to improve the quality of care in our center.

If you have any questions about this, please talk to one of our staff members.

- If the parent's employer does not have such a plan, encourage the parent to ask the employer to consider starting one. Parents can ask for information about dependent care plans from their benefit department or from independent benefit consultants. See also IRS Publication 503: Child and Dependent Care Expenses.

- Centers should discuss dependent care plans with parents when they first enroll their children. If the parent and center agree, they may want to put language into their contract stating that the parents will spend all of their dependent care funds on the center.

Keeping Accurate Records

It is important for your center and parents to share accurate records about the spending of dependent care funds. In order to avoid disagreements later about how much was spent, follow these steps:

Parents should not expect centers to sign blank receipts. Both parties should make sure the amount listed on the receipt is the correct amount.

It is reasonable for a center to receive payment before signing a receipt. This may not always be possible. But if a center signs a receipt and doesn't get paid, they may have a difficult time explaining to the IRS why this money shouldn't be included as income to the center.

Give parents a receipt at the end of the year indicating how much they paid for child care services. Have the parent sign the receipt, give them a copy, and keep a copy for your records.

It is important that the records of the parents and the center match. If the parent reports spending more from the dependent care plan than the center actually received, this could cause an audit of the parent and the center. Because parents may use more than one child care program during the year, it is doubly important that parent and center records match.

Looking Forward to 1994

Centers should consider these ideas for 1994:

- Some parents may be able to afford their current child care arrangement only because of the tax savings they received by participating in a dependent care plan. Other parents have more money in their pockets because of such plans and may be able to afford to pay more for child care. Centers may want to take this into consideration in setting their rates during the new year.

- Ask parents who can afford it to set aside more money in their plan for 1994 than they expect to pay for child care, with the understanding that the center will receive a "bonus." It costs parents less to give your center money through their plan than it does for them to give it to you after taxes have already been paid on it.

- Offer an employer-provided dependent care plan for your center employees.

What have you got to lose if you approach parents about any of the ideas in this article? Remember, if you don't ask for something, you can't expect to get it.

Note: This article is not providing legal, tax, or other professional services. Parents who don't follow the rules of their employer's dependent care plan may create a risk for themselves and their employer of being penalized by the IRS. Centers should advise parents to check with their employer dependent care plan operation before giving centers a "bonus."

Teaching Family Child Care Record Keeping and Tax Preparation

Market Your Tax Services to Family Child Care Providers
by Tom Copeland, JD

—Originally published in *Enrolled Agents Journal*, January/February 1997

In my frequent contact with family child care providers in the past five years, I have observed an increasing number of providers seeking tax preparers rather than doing their own tax returns. Enrolled Agents have a growing opportunity to expand their business by reaching out to these taxpayers.

This article suggests ways to identify family child care providers in your area and attract them as new clients. It also looks at the services you can offer to give your business an edge over the competition.

Family Child Care Market

Family child care providers are people who work from their own home caring for children. According to a recent study, 18 percent of all children under the age of six who are enrolled in a child care program are in family child care. Over 200,000 providers are state regulated, with significant variation in the regulation rules from state to state. Probably at least another million providers are caring for children without being regulated, either because they care for only one or two children and aren't required to be regulated, or because they are operating illegally.

Regulated family child care providers are almost exclusively women, usually caring for three to eight children other than their own. They tend to earn relatively little income from their business. According to a forthcoming Final Report of the Economics of Family Child Care Study by Kathy Modigliani and others, the average gross income of providers is $21,189. Incomes, however, vary greatly. The average income of the top 20 percent of providers is $39,908. Many providers have a working spouse and thus a larger family income.

Reaching the Providers

Family child care providers tend to be difficult to find. Lists of regulated providers available from state government offices are usually not useful because they are often out-of-date due to high turnover in the field. In order to effectively identify providers to market your services, Enrolled Agents should work through one of the three networks listed below. Almost every regulated family child care provider is actively connected to one of these three networks.

Child Care Resources and Referral Agencies (CCR&R) help parents find child care programs. They maintain a list (often on computer) of all regulated (and sometimes unregulated) child care programs in their areas. Usually there is one CCR&R in each city. In more rural areas, one agency may cover several counties. CCR&Rs have the most up-to-date list of regulated providers. Sometimes these lists may be purchased for a fee. Many CCR&Rs conduct training workshops, send out newsletters, or send out listings of tax preparers when providers request them.

To find out how to contact your local CCR&R, look in your local phone book under "Day Care" or "Child Care," or call your local county social service office or the national Association of Child Care Resource and Referral Agencies (202-393-5501) and ask for the name of your local agency.

Child and Adult Care Food Program (CACFP) sponsors reimburse providers for serving nutritious food. The Food Program is run by the U.S. Department of Agriculture. Each state has a number of local CACFP sponsors who serve providers locally. There may be several sponsors in the same area competing with each other because the sponsor gets paid according to how many providers they serve. A provider can only be served by one sponsor.

Sponsors visit the homes of each provider on their program several times a year. Sponsors often conduct workshops and publish newsletters. Providers read these newsletters fairly closely because they want to continue receiving the reimbursements. To contact the local sponsors in you area, call your local CCR&R.

There are thousands of Family Child Care Associations across the country. These are usually small groups of providers (50 to 200) who meet regularly and act as trade organizations to promote the interests of their members. They often hold monthly meetings and publish newsletters. There may be more than one local association in your area. To find the names of these associations, call the National Association of Family Child Care (800-628-9163).

Contact Checklist

Enrolled Agents should consider approaching all three of these networks in a similar manner:

- Offer to conduct a workshop on tax issues at local meetings or regional or state conferences.

- Set up a booth at local family child care conferences.

- Write an article or regular column on tax tips or run an advertisement in the associations' newsletters.

- Attend some of the local association meetings to introduce yourself and become recognized.

- Offer to be a local resource on tax matters and answer question on the phone.

- Provide a discount for your services to members of these networks.

Family child care providers can sometimes be intimidated by tax preparers, particularly if the tax preparer is a man. To overcome this, Enrolled Agents should introduce themselves to as many providers as possible and tell them that they are available to answer questions now and in the future. Establishing a long-term relationship with individuals and these networks is necessary to make providers comfortable with you.

Organizing Provider Records

One of the biggest problems Enrolled Agents have with family child care clients is having to take a lot of time sorting out unorganized records. Some providers may come to a tax preparer with well-organized tax records, but many do not. Here are some suggestions to help correct this problem.

Some tax preparers have developed their own intake form specifically for family child care providers that helps providers organize their records at tax time. A commercially developed one, "Day Care Income and Expense Worksheet," is available from Sauk Rapids Forms (612-722-5166).

There are three key record-keeping tasks that family child care providers should track throughout the year:

- Record the number of hours the home is used for business (particularly hours when the children in care are not present).

- Save all food receipts (even personal food receipts).

- Identify which purchases for the business are used 100 percent for the business and which are used both for business and personal purposes.

There are several family child care calendar and record-keeping publications on the market that can help providers better organize these and other business records. The *Calendar-Keeper* published by Redleaf Press is one example (see at right).

Teaching Family Child Care Record Keeping and Tax Preparation

JANUARY ATTENDANCE AND PAYMENT LOG

To record drop-off and pick-up times that vary, try using two lines per child, or consider purchasing the larger calendar with 30 lines.

CHILD'S NAME	S M T W T F S 1 2	TOTAL	S M T W T F S 3 4 5 6 7 8 9	TOTAL	S M T W T F S 10 11 12 13 14 15 16	TOTAL	S M T W T F S 17 18 19 20 21 22 23	TOTAL	S M T W T F S 24 25 26 27 28 29 30	TOTAL	S M 31	TOTAL
WEEKLY PAYMENT TOTALS												

MEAL COUNT TALLY

Total number of each meal served		
Include non-reimbursed meals	BREAKFASTS	
	LUNCHES	
	SNACKS	
	SUPPERS	
Date Food Program Claim Sent	Received	

	CACFP INCOME REC'D	OTHER INCOME REC'D	PARENT FEE INCOME REC'D
JANUARY INCOME			
BALANCE FORWARD			
TOTAL Y-T-D INCOME BY CATEGORY			

=	JAN TOTAL	
—	BALANCE FWD TOTAL	
=	TOTAL Y-T-D	

HOUSE EXPENSES WORKSHEET

YEAR:	Natural Gas		Electricity		Water/Sewer		Trash Collection			House Insurance		Real Estate Taxes		Mortgage Interest or Rent		House Repairs and Maintenance	
	Date Paid	Amount	Date Paid	Amount	Date Paid	Amount	Date Paid	Amount		Date Paid	Amount	Date Paid	Amount	Date Paid	Amount	Date Paid	Amount
JANUARY																	
FEBRUARY																	
MARCH																	
APRIL																	
MAY																	
JUNE																	
JULY																	
AUGUST																	
SEPTEMBER																	
OCTOBER																	
NOVEMBER																	
DECEMBER																	
TOTAL																	
TIME-SPACE PERCENTAGE																	
FCC BUSINESS EXPENSE																	

NOTE: You are entitled to claim a portion of these house expenses for your business. Use this worksheet to record these expenses each month or once a year. For each column, fill in the totals and your Time-Space percentage (to compute, see *The Basic Guide to Family Child Care Record Keeping*). To arrive at the FCC Business Expense, multiply the total in each column by the Time-Space percentage. Add together the FCC Business Expenses for Natural Gas, Electricity, Water/Sewer, and Trash Collection and enter the total under "Utilities" on the next page. Take the totals of the other FCC Business Expense columns and enter them on the next page. When you file your taxes, the house expenses on this page go directly onto **Form 8829 Expenses for Business Use of Your Home**.

57

As a way to save time, some tax preparers bring all their family child care clients together for a meeting to cover specialized issues. For example, rather than spending a lot of time filling out payroll forms for each client, a tax preparer in Minnesota could hold a meeting of her family child care clients once a year where she teaches them how to fill out payroll forms. The clients fill out the W-2 and W-3 forms at the meeting under the direct supervision of the tax preparer.

Often Enrolled Agents find themselves having to correct a taxpayer's problem that might have been avoided if the taxpayer had contacted the Enrolled Agent sooner. The three areas where this is an issue in family child care are sale of the home, hiring helpers (family member or nonfamily members), and going out of business. Many negative tax consequences can be avoided if the client discusses this early on with the Enrolled Agent.

Encourage your clients to contact you as soon as they begin thinking that any of these three events are a possibility. Put notices about this in your own newsletter or emphasize this point when speaking to an audience or family child care providers.

Gaining an Edge

The key to promoting your services to family child care providers is communicating clearly that you understand their business. (See "The Unique Business of Family Child Care" by the same author in the Spring 1996 *Enrolled Agents Journal*.) Stressing your years of tax preparation experience or your affiliation with a large organization is generally not considered meaningful to most providers. If you currently have very few family child care clients, emphasize that you have experience doing other small business tax returns and that you understand the difference between other businesses and family child care.

You may also want to consider ways to offer additional services to potential or current family child care clients. Because of the particularly difficult issues many family child care providers must handle, offering such services can distinguish you from your competition and can attract new business. Such services could include the following:

- Set up medical reimbursement plans for providers who hire their spouse or children. Such plans can save a provider's family a significant amount of taxes by claiming medical expenses as a business deduction.

- Set up a system to handle federal and state payroll tax forms for providers. This is an area where many providers do not follow the law because they often receive bad advice. Enrolled Agents should emphasize that they understand the rules for hiring family and nonfamily members and can help providers take advantage of the tax savings if the proper forms are filled out.

- Help providers understand the importance of setting up family budgets and saving money for retirement. This is a good topic for workshops at provider association meetings. Many providers need assistance with some basic financial planning. Promote the idea of providers establishing their own Simplified Employee Pension (SEP). Show them how they can reduce their current taxes and save for their retirement by using this plan.

- Help providers who are audited. Promote yourself as someone who can assist a provider in an audit. This is a good way to attract attention to yourself and gain a positive reputation in the local family child care community.

Summary

Although individual family child care providers may not generate significant revenue, Enrolled Agents who specialize in this area can expect to build up a significant number of new clients. Providers are looking for help, and the news that you are a tax preparer who understand this business will spread quickly by word of mouth. Keep the following highlights from this article in mind as you build your client base:

- Family child care providers offer Enrolled Agents a growing business opportunity.

- Almost every regulated family child care provider is actively connected to one of three professional networks.

- Family child care providers can sometimes be intimidated by tax preparers, particularly if the tax preparer is a man.

- There are three key record-keeping tasks that family child care providers should track throughout the year.

- The key to promoting your services to family child care providers is communicating clearly that you understand their business.

How to Use Form 3115 to Deduct Previously Unclaimed Depreciation
by Tom Copeland, JD, and Don Gilbo

—Originally published in *Tax Practitioners Journal*, Spring 1997

The issuing of IRS Revenue Procedure 96-31 last summer should make a significant, positive impact on the thousands of taxpayers who have not claimed all of the business depreciation deductions they were entitled to in earlier years. Before this revenue procedure, many taxpayers and tax preparers often failed to take depreciation deductions because of various reasons and then later came to the realization that these deductions were allowed or allowable. This new change now makes using depreciation rules more practical and profitable.

The revenue procedure allows taxpayers to deduct previously unclaimed depreciation by filing Form 3115: Application for Change in Accounting Method. The property must be depreciable under section 167, 168 (ACRS), 168 (MACRS), or 197. The taxpayer must not have previously taken any allowable depreciation or have taken less than the amount allowable. To deduct previously unclaimed depreciation in 1997, there are five major guidelines. The taxpayer must:

1) Be in business in 1997 (even if only for part of the year).

2) Own the property they wish to depreciate in 1997. The taxpayer can sell the property later in 1997 without adversely affecting their Form 3115 deductions.

3) Be using the property for their business in 1997.

4) File Form 3115 on or before the 180th day of the tax year that the taxpayer wants to claim the deductions. The 1997 deadline is June 29, 1997. If the year is a short year, file Form 3115 before the end of the short year or on the 180th day, whichever is earlier.

5) Claim the depreciation deductions by filing a timely Form 1040 (including extensions) for 1997.

Taxpayers who will be most likely to take advantage of this revenue procedure are those who own rental property, those who claim the home office deduction, and the self-employed, particularly family child care providers. There are a large number of items that may not have been previously depreciated by a taxpayer that are prime candidates for including on Form 3115:

• The house, home improvements (new furnaces, roof, remodeling projects, room additions, fixtures, etc.), and land improvements (fences, driveways, landscaping, etc.).

• Personal property such as computers, printers, desks, tables, chairs, file cabinets, furniture, and appliances.

• Property that was owned by the taxpayer before the business began and then used in the business.

• Farm property such as pole barns, water pump houses, etc.

Obviously, a particular item must be a legitimate business expense for it to be entitled to a depreciation deduction. In the field of family child care, there are scores of items that meet this test (washer, dryer, freezer, refrigerator, beds, sofas, outdoor play equipment, etc.).

What should be done if the taxpayer has no receipts for the undepreciated property? Have the taxpayer search for other records, such as credit card statements, canceled checks, and repair service contracts. Also, take pictures of the property. Copy recent ads that describe the property and list its price. The most important point for property owned before the business began is to have some proof that the taxpayer did own the property at the time the business began. Use the lower of the fair market value or the adjusted basis of the property to claim the depreciation deduction. At a recent audit, one of the authors of this article presented photos of previously undepreciated property along with an estimate of its fair market value. The auditor accepted the estimates without requiring the original receipts.

Using Form 3115

Tax preparers must follow specific depreciation rules when claiming expenses using Form 3115. Normally a taxpayer must make an election to use straight-line depreciation rules in the first year the property was used in the business. If this is the case, the MACRS accelerated depreciation rules must be used to claim deductions on Form 3115. If the taxpayer didn't have the choice to elect to use straight-line rules in the first year the property was used for business, then the taxpayer must use the rules that were originally required. Here is a breakdown of the rules that must be used when claiming depreciation using Form 3115:

* Home: nonresidential real property, 39-year (or 31.5-year) straight-line.

* Home improvement: nonresidential real property, 39-year (or 31.5-year) straight-line.

* Land improvement: asset class 00.3 land improvement, 15-year 150% declining balance.

* Computer: asset class 00.12 information systems. If used 50% or less in business, 5-year straight-line. If used more that 50% in business, 5-year MACRS 200% declining balance.

* Other personal property: asset class 00.11 office furniture, fixtures, and equipment, 7-year MACRS 200% declining balance.

* Car: asset class 00.22 automobiles, 5-year MACRS 200% declining balance.

Note: MACRS depreciation rules did not exist before 1987. For the rules on how to depreciate property used in your business before 1987, consult IRS Publication 534: Depreciating Property Places in Service Before 1987.

Tax preparers should think of unclaimed depreciation for their self-employed clients as one of two types: Schedule C depreciation (furniture, computer, appliances, and other personal property) and Form 8829 depreciation (home and home improvements). Calculate how much of each type of depreciation your client was entitled to deduct for each unclaimed year. Higher Schedule C or Form 8829 depreciation deductions from Form 3115 may affect the ability to claim some deductions in the current year. Also, note that Form 8829 was first introduced in 1991. The rules before then, however, were the same regarding the limitation of claiming home office expenses that create a business loss.

Showing a Loss

Can deducting previously unclaimed depreciation create a loss on Schedule C? Yes and no. Depreciation of personal property can always be used to claim a loss for a business. Depreciation of a home or home improvements cannot. Tax preparers must follow the regular rules regarding carrying forward disallowed depreciation expenses.

When filing Form 3115 with the taxpayer's 1997 tax forms, enter all Schedule C depreciation from Form 3115 onto the 1997 Schedule C, line 27, "Other Expenses." Write "Section 481(a) Adjustment" next to the amount on one of the blank lines under Part V of Schedule C. Note that this may cause some of the original Form 8829 expenses to be disallowed. Enter all

Form 8829 depreciation from Form 3115 onto the 1997 Form 8829, line 29, "Carryover of Excess Casualty Losses and Depreciation." Enter "Section 481(a) Adjustment" on this line. Follow the regular instructions to Form 8829 regarding the deduction limitation rules. Some expenses may have to be carried forward to the 1998 Form 8829.

Let's look at an example. Suppose the original 1997 Schedule C showed a $1,000 profit and the original 1997 Form 8829 showed a total of $500 in deductions. If Form 3115 (filed in 1997) had $2,000 in Schedule C depreciation and $1,500 in Form 8829 depreciation (home and home improvements), how much of this depreciation could be claimed in 1997? First, claim all $2,000 in Schedule C depreciation on the 1997 Schedule C, line 27. This creates a tentative loss of $1,000 on the Schedule C. But the original $500 Form 8829 expenses shown on Schedule C cannot create a loss, so this amount must be put back on Form 8829 and carried over to the 1998 Form 8829. The new total for the 1997 Schedule C shows a $500 loss. Next, put the $1,500 in Form 8829 depreciation from Form 3115 on line 29 of the 1997 Form 8829. Since this amount also cannot create or add to a loss, add it to the $500 that will be carried forward to the 1998 Form 8829. Thus, a total of $2000 will be carried forward to the 1998 Form 8829, line 29, "Carryover of Excess Casualty Losses and Depreciation."

Special note for owners of rental property: Tax preparers should ask their clients with rental property if they have been deducting all allowable depreciation for their rental property, including any furnishings. Previously unclaimed depreciation should be reported on Schedule E, line 18, "Other." Write "Section 481(a) Adjustment" next to one of the blank lines.

In the above examples, we have used line numbers as they appear on the 1996 IRS forms. They may differ on forms in later years.

Final Notes

- There is no filing fee to file Form 3115.

- Tax preparers should take into account that showing a lower business profit after filing Form 3115 may impact the eligibility of the taxpayer for the earned income credit. Some taxpayers may be able to get a higher credit and some may receive less.

- Tax preparers should be assertive in asking their clients whether all allowable depreciation deductions were claimed in earlier years. Using this new revenue procedure presents a major opportunity to reduce the tax burden of your clients.

Teaching Family Child Care Record Keeping and Tax Preparation

Attention Trainers and Tax Preparers

We hope you have found this training manual to be informative and useful. You may be interested to know that, as a family child care trainer, you can purchase quantities of Redleaf Press publications (*Calendar-Keeper, The Basic Guide to Family Child Care Record Keeping, Tax Workbook*) at a discount. You can profitably resell these publications in your classes, or give them away to attendees as part of their class fees or to tax clients. For more information about this program, please call 651-641-6675.

Redleaf Press Titles

The Basic Guide to Family Child Care Record Keeping - Easy-to-follow instructions on how to keep all your family child care business records. This invaluable guide explains over 750 allowable business deductions.

The Business of Family Child Care with Tom Copeland - This video covers the seven most important record-keeping rules, tax tips, and a brief discussion of contracts and insurance.

Business Receipt Book - Receipts specifically for family child care payments improve your record keeping; 50 sets per book.

Calendar-Keeper - Activities, family child care record keeping, recipes, and more. Updated annually. Most popular publication in the field.

Calendar-Keeper Software - A comprehensive software program that can handle all of your record-keeping needs. It contains sections on Food Program management, detailed expense tracking, and dozens of reports and worksheets to help you organize your business.

Family Child Care Contracts and Policies - Sample contracts and policies and how-to information on using them effectively to improve your business.

Family Child Care Tax Workbook - Updated every year, latest step-by-step information on forms, depreciation, and tax law changes.

Mileage-Keeper - This mileage log book for business vehicles shows providers exactly how to keep the proper records to claim business expenses.

Room for Loving, Room for Learning: Finding the Space You Need in Your Family Child Care Home - Take control of the space in your home and create a warm, stimulating place for children. Filled with great ideas for play areas and storage.

Sharing in the Caring - This packet of agreement forms and other information helps establish good relationships between providers and parents.

Teaching Family Child Care Record Keeping and Tax Preparation: A Curriculum for Trainers (Book and Cassettes) - Now you can hear Tom Copeland deliver his popular workshop on record keeping and tax preparation. The tapes and book will work well for trainers and providers.

Tips From Tina - Over 500 tips for hassle-free child care in one exhaustive resource for you, a busy provider.

To order or for more information, call Redleaf Press

800-423-8309